Opening My Cultural Lens

A Globe Trekker's Experiences and Photographs

GAIL SHORE

Opening My Cultural Lens: A Globe Trekker's Experiences and Photographs
© 2023 by Gail Shore

All rights reserved. No part of this book may be reproduced in any form whatsoever, by photography or xerography or by any other means, by broadcast or transmission, by translation into any kind of language, nor by recording electronically or otherwise, without permission in writing from the author, except by a reviewer, who may quote brief passages in critical articles or reviews.

Edited by Kerry Stapley
Cover and interior photographs by the author
Book design and typesetting by Dan Pitts
Managing Editor: Laurie Buss Herrmann

ISBN 13: 978-1-64343-730-9
Library of Congress Catalog Number: 2022906177
Printed in the United States of America
First Edition: 2023
27 26 25 24 23   5 4 3 2 1

Beaver's Pond Press
939 West Seventh Street
Saint Paul, MN 55102
(952) 829-8818
www.BeaversPondPress.com

To order, visit www.GailShore.com.

Contact Gail Shore at www.GailShore.com for speaking engagements, book club discussions, and interviews.

To everyone who encouraged and supported me
throughout my life,
except for my guidance counselor,
who told me I should be a secretary or a housewife

Contents

Introduction: Turning Passion into Purpose 1
From Here to Timbuktu: What's Your Favorite Place? 9
I'm Not a Tourist: Preparation 17
Kenya: My First Safari 21
Japan: "Immersing" in a New Culture 25
Turkey: Lake Wobegon No More 31
Russia: Jiffy Pop and the KGB 37
Vietnam: Following the War of My Generation 45
Nepal: One Foot in Front of the Other 51
Peru & Galápagos: Inca Dinka Do 63
Papua New Guinea: Some Things I Can't Tell My Mother 69
Bhutan: I Thought I Could Be a Buddhist 79
Tibet: Rooftop of the World 87
China: Before Gucci Gotcha 93
Egypt: How'd You Get So Funky? 103
Amazon: Yes, It Was Me. I Disrupted the Ecosystem 111
Guatemala: I Speak Fluent Pantomime 129
Cuba: Che, Castro, and Hemingway's Bartender 135
India: Two-Sided Mirror 143
Cambodia & Laos: When the World Stopped 157
Rwanda: Weren't You Scared? Part One 167
Nicaragua: Weren't You Scared? Part Two 173
Ghana: The Door of No Return 177

Morocco: Rock the Kasbah 187
Jordan & Lebanon: I Wonder What They're Saying
About Me Now 197
Namibia: Do You Live as Well in Your Land? 209
Israel: In the Cradle of Humankind 221
Mongolia: What's on Tap? 233
The Stans of Central Asia: Stranger in a Strange Land 241
Syria: Hospitality of Strangers 251
Myanmar: Land of Contradictions 261
Mali: Too Close to Danger 271
North Korea: One-Sided Mirror 279
Iran: Another Cultural Faux Pas 289
Tanzania: My Last Safari—Coming Full Circle 301
Close: If I Could Visit My Younger Self 311

Acknowledgments 315
Discussion Questions 319

Everybody should come here.
Everyone should see how complicated, how deeply troubled,
and yet at the same time, beautiful and awesome the world can be.
Everyone should experience, even as the clouds gather,
what's at stake, what could be lost, what's still here.

—Anthony Bourdain,
travel documentarian and host of *Anthony Bourdain: Parts Unknown*

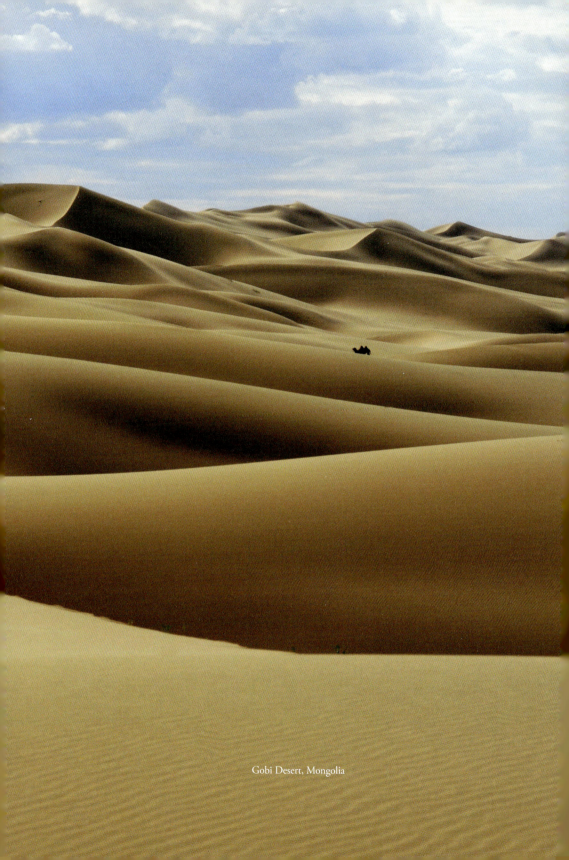
Gobi Desert, Mongolia

INTRODUCTION

Turning Passion into Purpose

In the '60s, the only person of color at my Milwaukee-suburban high school was an exchange student from Thailand. His name was Pradit. He was from a foreign land, making him different, we presumed, from the rest of us. Pradit's last name was so long that few of us could pronounce it, and sadly, fewer tried.

Today's schools look entirely different than when I was a teenager. Hundreds of languages are now spoken in hallways and cafeterias, and classrooms include many people like Pradit.

In lieu of my homogenous upbringing, I'm often asked how I became so absorbed in global cultures. Like many others in my hometown of Milwaukee, I came from a blue-collar, working-class family. Our only adventure was making sure I didn't get car sick in the back seat of the Chevy when we crowded in to visit relatives up north every few years. We never traveled by air. We rarely went anywhere at all, probably because of the car-sick thing.

Opening My Cultural Lens

My mom and dad were loving, hard-working parents who instilled in us some basic life lessons, including responsibility, work ethic, honesty, money management, and good manners. (The good manners part took a bit longer.) Try as they did, they couldn't change the fact that I was growing up in an environment that offered girls few career options, none of which appealed to me. So, I had no plans. There was not much on my horizon.

For example, during my senior year of high school, I remember my guidance counselor giving me his best career advice. He sat at a table. I stood in front of him. For the entire meeting, which didn't last but for a few minutes, I remained standing. The way he saw it, I had three choices. One: become a teacher—a very odd recommendation for someone who was, let's just say, an *unfocused* student. Two: become a nurse—an even more puzzling option given that science and math were indisputably my two worst subjects. And three: become a housewife. Wait, what? Did he just say that out loud? Oh, good Lord, what a time for girls. Needless to say, I left that "meeting" with little guidance.

I did attempt to go to college—with no recommended major or path in mind—but left early with no better understanding of what I was supposed to do or what I wanted to do. I didn't recognize the op-

Gail, a 10-year-old Girl Scout, sadly never earned her Homemaking badge.

portunities available to me in those days, nor do I recall any sense of direction or advice from my teachers. So, of course, I failed to connect with my studies and did not do well. Those were not my favorite years. I just didn't know where I fit.

But luck, pure luck, was around the corner. No, I did not become a housewife.

My life was about to change forever when I landed a job working for a small airline—a job that not only provided a paycheck, but, more importantly, offered travel benefits: inexpensive tickets whose value would turn out to be incalculable. In 1967, I went to work at North Central, which became Republic, and then Northwest. In all, I spent twenty years spread between Milwaukee, New Orleans, and Minneapolis. Those days were some of the most exciting of my life. They were also, on a number of levels, the most transformational.

As a new airline employee, I was given travel passes, which felt like an extended hand to an open map. I hardly knew where to begin. I didn't travel alone then, but rather, got together with fellow employees—all young and single—to figure out where we'd jet to with little cash and only a weekend to spend. The trips were superficial, to be sure. I never set out to accomplish anything other than to see cities our family's Chevy hadn't reached. I couldn't rub two nickels together, but I was having fun cracking open a strange new world. Soon, these trips included travel out of the country.

My first trip overseas was in 1968. I went to Switzerland, and while it lasted just a few days, I saw the glorious Alps, heard folks speaking different languages, spent a different currency, and toured the popular sites. Back in those days, we flew by the seat of our pants. We never had overnight accommodations or car rentals planned. We just figured out all that stuff when we arrived. That, alone, was an adventure. Luckily, those days were safer; it was a different world than today. That kind of travel taught us a lot about risk-taking, decision-making, and responsibility. Traveling was beginning to dramatically transform me from a Midwestern girl who had no vision for the near term, never mind the future, into a curious adult who couldn't wait to see what each new day might bring.

For years, my trips continued to more conventional places. But that all changed in the early '80s when I finally took a proper vacation and went on an African safari. It was a journey ripped from the pages of *National Geographic*: the wild and diverse landscapes; the Maasais' painted faces, colorful clothing, and beaded jewelry; and the animals . . . oh, the animals! That experience had a profound effect on my travels to come. That's also when I realized I needed to buy a serious camera and teach myself how to use it. I could not go to Africa with an Instamatic.

In those early years, I held a number of different customer service and sales jobs at the airline. Eventually, I became a district sales manager, which brought me to New Orleans. One day, while sitting at my desk finalizing my Mardi Gras costume, I received a call from the airline's public relations director in Minneapolis. Out of the blue, Redmond—everybody called him Red—asked me to join the PR department to run its tourism and travel writer programs. I was flabbergasted, and again, wholly unaware that this job would change my life. No thanks to my high school guidance counselor, public relations became my career path. Red became my mentor, the only such person I've ever had. He taught me so much and supported my involvement in community and industry organizations. He also encouraged me to return to college to get a bachelor's in communications, which I earned while working full time in the department.

A few years later, after yet another merger (airline mergers were the thing back then), I left the airline. While I missed the benefits, my traveling days were far from over. In fact, they'd just begun. My wonder had been piqued, and I was intrigued by destinations that were culturally distinct—faraway places that most people never visit.

I began to travel alone. Because I'm a party of one, my trips are

Introduction

A door open to the world

certainly more expensive, but they're also customized—no groups, no bus tours. Just me, always with a private, hired guide for safety and access. I'm not drawn to areas of conflict, but because I've been to remote locations, I've stumbled into some precarious situations.

For decades, I've saved and invested as much as possible into exploring locations whose fragile cultures and environments are at risk. Using the word *invested* is quite intentional. Over the years, by investing my time and savings into global adventures, the returns have influenced my life beyond measure.

That's not to say my trips are easy. I spend a lot of time praying for electricity, hot water, and sit-down toilets. I can also admit to being an unadventurous eater, but I figure if you fry something long enough, it becomes edible—even bugs and other local delights. Those inconveniences have never stopped me from experiencing some extraordinary journeys. Plus, they make good stories.

As my solo trips progressed, I realized others—a lot of others—were keenly interested in my excursions. These were places and cultures others know little about, so I began to share my photos and stories—my lens to the world. I gave presentations and slideshows and showed my photography at art galleries and art fairs. People told me how my experiences sparked their interest in geography and history, as well as current events, geopolitical issues, and human rights. I never expected this! My wanderlust, which began as my own personal window and mirror, was growing into something much broader. Something transformational was happening; I was turning passion into purpose and setting a place *for myself* at a new table.

Fast forward to 2005 when, at the encouragement of friends and colleagues, I founded a nonprofit using my photography and experiences to promote understanding and respect for all people. Cultural Jambalaya creates free, online programming that educators use to spark students' curiosity and broaden their world views right in the classroom.

I am so fortunate to have experienced so many of our planet's incredible gifts and to have met the most unforgettable people. Yet, it's what those strangers have taught *me* that has opened my own aperture and given my life more texture. Most importantly, I've learned that when we discover each other's similarities, we can begin to respect each other's differences. I often think about my high school's foreign exchange student, wishing I could have apologized to Pradit for not doing a better job of welcoming him into our school community. I'd also like to assure him that while we have a long, long way to go, there are many initiatives today in America that promote the importance of diversity, equity, and inclusion of all individuals.

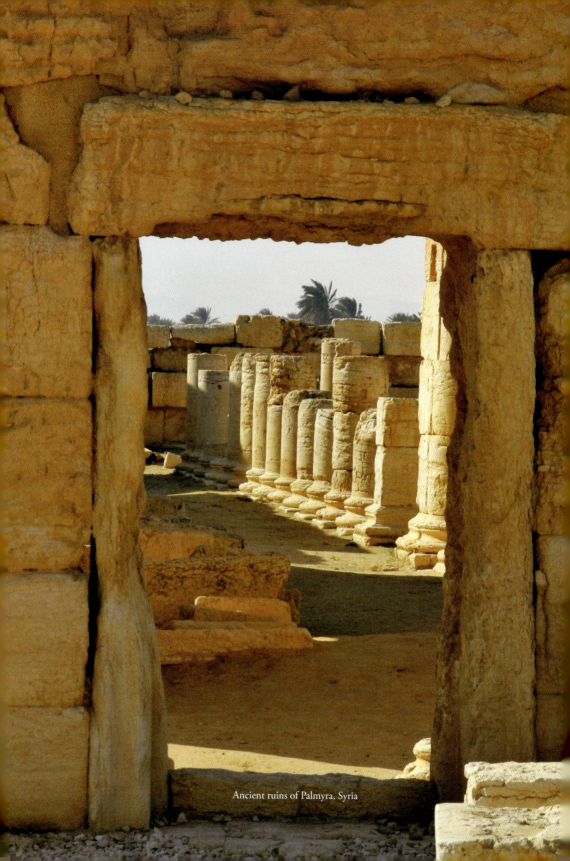
Ancient ruins of Palmyra, Syria

FROM HERE TO TIMBUKTU

What's Your Favorite Place?

What's your favorite place? I get that question all the time. It's like naming a favorite child. The answer is all of them, because each has shown me something new and inspiring, remarkable and fascinating, and certainly thought-provoking.

I've photographed countless World Heritage sites and wonders of the world: mountains from the Himalayas to the Andes; The Red Sea, Yellow Sea, and Black Sea; and rivers including the Yangtze, Sepik, Ganges, and Mekong. I've captured sunrises at Mount Everest and Mt. Fuji, as well as in expansive deserts such as the Sahara and Gobi, where, from the tops of dunes, I watched it rise. I've shot sunsets at the Perito Moreno Glacier and the Great Rift Valley.

Upsala Glacier, Patagonia

Opening My Cultural Lens

Sunrise on the Sahara

My jaw drops every time I see the miracles of nature: Bengal tigers in India, blue-footed boobies in the Galápagos, mountain gorillas in Rwanda, Magellanic penguins in Chile, black rhinos, and Africa's Great Wildebeest Migration. And then—oh, man—holding in my arms a precious baby panda in China.

From Here to Timbuktu

Blue-footed booby, Galapagos

Mountain gorilla, Rwanda

Observing unique religious ceremonies and activities has enriched my own spirituality. I've been blessed by Buddhist monks, Hindu monks, and Muslim imams; I've participated in traditional healing ceremonies with shamans and medicine men. I've witnessed Jewish rituals at the Western Wall, the Christian penitent of magdarame in the Philippines, Hindu weddings in India, Ramadan throughout the Middle East, and spiritual festivals around the world.

Certainly, the rarest trip was an extraordinary peek inside North Korea, where I crossed the DMZ and sat in official Democratic People's Republic of Korea government seats to watch the unforgettable Mass Games. I've drunk vodka with members of the KGB, tea with the Tuareg, schnapps with a headman in Ghana, and chicha with a whole lot of village chiefs in the Amazon.

Gail holding a young panda in China.

Mass Games, North Korea

Opening My Cultural Lens

How can I have a favorite?

Many adventures have introduced me to native cultures I would otherwise have only seen in *National Geographic*. In Myanmar, I spent several days in the mountains photographing the remarkable Chin women who tattoo their faces, then danced with an isolated tribe that had not seen a westerner since before World War II. On the border of Angola, I photographed the fascinating Himba women who cover their skin with red ochre, and in remote Papua New Guinea, I shared a meal with an indigenous family who had never touched the hand of a white person. And I've treasured random acts of kindness and unexpected hospitality from strangers everywhere I've gone.

Tattooed Chin woman, Myanmar

I've been followed and surveilled in Iran, Turkmenistan, Myanmar, North Korea, and most probably, in other places when I was not even aware it was going on. The more I've traveled, the more I've

Himba woman, Namibia	Sing-Sing ceremony, Papua New Guinea

learned about some of the most horrifying atrocities in human history, such as the Holocaust, South Africa's Apartheid, Cambodia's Killing Fields, Laos' Secret War which attempted to exterminate Hmong people, Africa's horrifying slave trade, brutal civil wars, and unspeakable genocides. And I got a little bit too close to being a victim of terrorism in Mali.

Yet, my memories also include priceless moments of hope and joy. In Port-au-Prince, I held a Haitian child whose life would forever change the next day when she'd undergo a procedure to repair her cleft lip and palate. The birth defect affected her speech and facial structure. In some cultures, people believe demons are to blame for the defect, resulting in families and communities ostracizing, abandoning, and even killing an innocent child.

Prayer flags, Bhutan

Here's my moment of Zen:

The most out-of-this-world moment I've ever had in my life happened in north Queensland in Australia. I was spearfishing on a river late one night with a couple of Aboriginal fellows. Scattered clouds covered the moon, and millions of stars brightened the midnight sky. One of my Aussie mates sat in the stern of the boat by the motor, steering us forward, waiting for the tide to drop to make it easier to spearfish. The lead guy stood at the bow, shining a large spotlight at the water. It captured dozens of pairs of crocodile eyes, which glared ominously at us as we passed.

Be still, I told myself. *This is no time to rock the boat.*

Regrettably, on this night, I had left my camera behind. I figured it would just get in the way or get wet while spearfishing. It was a big mistake.

As I stood carefully to receive direction on how to hold the long spear, the clouds began to drift away from the moon, revealing a rare, optical weather phenomenon, not even my Aboriginal pals had ever seen. The moon was encircled by six distinct colored rings: blue, white, yellow, red, magenta, and green, with a seventh circle of light around them all. It looked like a circular rainbow.

I learned later it was called a lunar corona. Colorful rings, like halos, are created when the moonlight is diffracted by an extremely thin cloud. It is so unusual because the water droplets which form the cloud must be perfectly uniform for this phenomenon to occur. We were gobsmacked! It was the most mesmerizing spectacle, and the three of us stared speechlessly in wonder. But it was real, and it was the closest thing to a spiritual moment I've ever had.

It's happenings and adventures like these that make it impossible for me to say which is my favorite place, coolest sight, luckiest photo, or most memorable moment. These cultural experiences have collectively changed me from an indifferent young girl into a curious global citizen.

My transformation came after years of witnessing several key lessons:

- Happiness comes from family, faith, and community. Many people who live within the most basic, modest means don't need all the stuff that *we think* makes us happy.

- The Golden Rule. Religions and spiritualities around the world are based on the same principle—treat others as you would like to be treated. It's inarguable and simple.

- We must never, ever take for granted our freedom and liberty, which are imperative to dignity and fundamental to joy. Freedom and liberty are our greatest blessings.

- And most importantly, while we all may look, dress, speak or pray differently, people everywhere are more alike than we are different. Understanding this is the path to compassion and empathy.

I'M NOT A TOURIST

Preparation

People ask me all the time how I plan for my excursions and who helps me. Preparations often begin a year out with a call to my longtime St. Paul travel agent, who has decades of experience and trusted global connections. My agent then partners with another firm specializing in the part of the world I'm headed to. They handle the day-to-day arrangements, including local transportation and lodging. Since my adventures are working trips, my agent makes sure everyone in route understands I am a traveler, not a tourist. I always have to make sure my passport contains extra pages for entry stamps and visas, and on occasion, I've needed letters of recommendation to gain permission to enter a country. This is usually true of places, which are to some degree, police states.

    The agency at my destination selects my guides; this is the single most important piece of planning for these types of trips. These agencies are familiar with my itinerary, and they fully understand my goals.

The guides are local experts who are well known and respected in their communities. Sometimes, they are village chiefs; sometimes, they're historians, and oftentimes, they are local government-issued guides who are also keeping an eye on me. Almost always, they are men. Being a guide is often considered a very respected job. Thus, in patriarchal societies, it is only offered to men. The thorough orchestration by these agencies helps me to maximize my time. But more importantly, they take every precaution to ensure my safety is not at risk.

My packing list, before digital photography, started out with my trusty old Canon AE-1 and dozens and dozens of rolls of Fujichrome 50-slide film. Seemingly overnight, digital cameras turned the visual world upside down in a good way. Needing to adapt, I got my first digital camera, a Canon EOS D30. How photography has evolved.

1995: Gail's fortune cookie

Long after other people carried mobile phones, I did not. Nor did I bring my laptop. I used these excursions as an opportunity to unplug. Early on, to communicate with people back home, I'd search for a fax machine. Later, I'd hunt down an Internet café to send messages to my sister. She'd typically receive calls and emails from family and friends wondering if I was still alive or if I had been arrested yet, so I always let her know that I was okay.

Most of my overnights have been at small, rural inns of various sorts. Some had cots and mosquito nets. Sometimes, places don't have hot water or reliable electricity. I've learned not to count on these amenities. I bring bug spray, permethrin, biodegradable soap, toilet paper, sometimes a water purifier, lots of trail mix, and a jar of Skippy. I always bring a headlamp. They're handy when negotiating squat-only outhouses in the middle of the night.

Finally, after an appointment at the travel clinic to get all the required medicines and shots, I'm good to go. Giddy-up.

Route of the End of the World

KENYA

My First Safari

Like many people, I started out with a long list of places on the board. By the time I turned thirty, I had been to nearly every country in Europe. Today, about a hundred countries (and fifty states) later, I have exhausted those lists over and over, hopscotching from here to the Middle East, Africa, Asia, Latin America, and back again—to and from destinations that are all culturally unique.

Before I began traveling alone, I took a couple of trips with my sister, Jean, who also worked in the airline industry and had her own passes. In 1982, we took a two-week vacation and headed to Kenya for a safari.

In Nairobi, we connected with our guide, whose Western name was Robert. He was a skinny young fellow who did not speak English. (Our bleak budget didn't include an English-speaking guide.) He picked us up in an older, red, four-door Fiat. (Our budget also didn't include a four-wheel drive, sightseeing vehicle). In spite of his youth, he was a gifted guide.

I knew we were in for something special when just minutes outside of Nairobi, we had to stop and yield to several giraffes that sauntered nonchalantly across the highway. It was jaw-dropping! Back home, I'd see deer cross the road all the time, but giraffes? I had to remind myself this was not a zoo; there were no fences. This was Africa, and those giraffes were only a glimpse of what was to come.

Male giraffes can be 20 feet tall.

It was just before Kenya's rainy season, and our dated Fiat did not keep out the fine dust. After hours of bouncing over dry roads, we were covered from head to toe with layers of dirt. At the end of our first day, I got out of the car, stood up, and sneezed. Like a cartoon, a cloud of dust shot out of my nose and ears. Our luggage, which was in the trunk, was unrecognizable.

Robert took us to the Maasai Mara National Reserve and Nakuru, one of the largest towns in Kenya, and up to Mount Kenya National Park. Then he circled south to Tsavo, Lake Amboseli, and Chyulu Hills. We learned about the traditions of Kenya's many ethnic tribes, especially the colorful and nomadic Maasai people. I kept thinking, here I was, roaming around in the middle of the Serengeti, photographing unique ethnic traditions and an endless array of wild animals—lions and rhinos and hippos, oh, my! I smiled as I imagined the narrating voice of Sir David Attenborough.

Masaai's high-fat diet consists primarily of cow's blood and milk.

Masaai's wealth is measured by their number of cattle and children.

Day after day, the amazing and unexpected would happen. We witnessed a wildebeest giving birth to a gangly youngster. Within minutes, it was forced onto its wobbly legs and attempted, frantically, to run—an instinctive skill necessary for its survival. Another day, we got stuck in the mud (which is not recommended in the middle of the Serengeti) with no one around to help except for a pack of lions, which circled and circled our seemingly vulnerable little car. In Swahili, Robert tried to assure us it was not dinner time and that they were just curious. You could've fooled me. The lions scrutinized us through the windows, sniffing around before thankfully strolling far enough away for us to hop out and quickly push the little red sedan out of the mud.

Robert seemed to see everything. He had a sixth sense and keen eye for camouflaged animals, which he pointed out to us as we struggled to locate what he was spotting. One late afternoon, he ever-so-slowly stopped the car because he spied a cheetah rising up on a large boulder. With the sun setting on the cheetah's magnificent face, we watched it stalk a topi, a common African antelope. Step by deliberate step, the cheetah gently crept up the rock, lowering its head and shoulders while keeping the topi in sight. We remained in suspense, waiting for it to leap, but for whatever reason, the cheetah decided not to pursue its prey.

Cheetah stalking a topi at dusk

Elephants can hear through their feet, sensing sound waves in the ground.

Without the interference of city lights, on clear nights, the stars were unlike anything I'd ever seen. There were millions, and they appeared so big and bright that I felt I could have touched them. One night we were returning to our cabin from dinner at the lodge. We were almost to our door when we saw an enormous elephant and her calf gnawing on some branches just feet away. Elephants can be extremely aggressive when frightened. Since they were right outside our door, we should have simply scooted inside—but no—Jean thought this would be an ideal time to take their picture. She carefully reached for her Instamatic and slowly walked toward the pair to get a better shot. It was not her best idea. Jean got just one step too close when the mother let out a thunderous trumpeting screech that signaled her distress. It was so loud I swear Jean leapt the few feet to the cabin door without touching the ground. As I learned later, trumpeting can be heard six miles away. Jean never got her picture.

JAPAN

"Immersing" in a New Culture

The next opportunity I had for an extended trip had to wait until 1987. I left the airline and, as a parting gift, they gave me one last international ticket and a gold pin. I had been recruited to take a PR position with the University of Minnesota and had some time to travel before the new job began. Over the years, I had enjoyed some abbreviated trips to Asia, and I wanted to get back. Japan was on my radar.

I began in Tokyo, one of the largest cities in the world. Today, its population is a staggering thirty-eight million people—six million more than when I was there in 1987. The sheer size of this enormous cosmopolitan city made it a challenge to see some of its key sites. But thanks to Tokyo's extensive and efficient transit system, I did my best in the limited time I had.

Japanese architecture is distinctive, and many designs feature wood structures with tiled or thatched roofs. Japanese buildings are always constructed in alignment with nature, maximizing light and using natural materials. Sunken entrance spaces (sort of like mudrooms) keep the interiors clean. Rooms are created by sliding doors and shoji screens that surround tatami-mat flooring.

Japan's characteristic architecture

There are countless temples and shrines in Tokyo, and I managed to visit as many as possible. In Japan, Buddhism and Shinto are culturally interconnected religions. Many Japanese people practice both. Shinto worships many gods and spirits of nature and wants our souls to live in harmony with the natural world. Buddhism is a religion of ethics and transcendence and uses disciplines like meditation to free us from human suffering and to achieve enlightenment.

Buddhist places of worship are called temples, whereas Shinto spaces for worship are shrines. I would enter the holy shrines through a torii gate. Then, it was customary to rinse my hands and mouth to purify my mind and body. I took a ladle in my right hand to wash my left, then reversed the process to wash my other hand. Finally, without using the ladle, I rinsed my mouth with the water and spit it out. At the temples, the faithful also light incense in the belief that the smoke has healing powers.

Torii gates mark the entrance to sacred Shinto shrines.

Incense is used for spirituality and meditation.

Of course, I took a train to the Ginza, Tokyo's iconic shopping district that is unquestionably one of the most exclusive shopping areas in the world. I slurped soba noodles at some of the ubiquitous sushi bars and relaxed at Ueno Park, a peaceful public oasis built in traditional Japanese style.

There was one more must-see Tokyo site I had heard so much about: The Tsukiji Fish Market. It is the most amazing fish market in the world, handling more than two thousand tons of seafood daily. I went in the early morning. It was already frantic as wholesale buyers eagerly paid top price at the famous tuna auction to satisfy their sushi-loving clients.

I wanted to see more of traditional Japan, especially Kyoto, so I took the bullet train to the ancient city, which was also famous for its temples, shrines, and imperial palaces. There, I learned about nightingale flooring, a security element built into the hallways of some of the ancient palaces to protect the emperors. Numerous boards were designed to creak, making chirping noises that would scare off uninvited guests sneaking around the hallways. Brilliant!

Kyoto is loaded with exquisite gardens designed to achieve harmony and serenity. Traditional Japanese gardens use natural aesthetics and ornamentation, including water, plants, and rocks, as design elements. I stopped often to sit on the benches, feeling my shoulders relax as I appreciated these tranquil settings and the sweet aroma of the cherry blossoms.

Japanese garden

Outside of Kyoto, I overnighted at a *ryokan*—a traditional inn. There, I experienced a Japanese style of hospitality called *omotenashi*. I was greeted by a personal attendant, who served all my meals, prepared my bed, and simply took care of me from the moment I arrived. Upon entering the ryokan, I took off my shoes and changed into slippers and an informal kimono. No English was spoken there.

I was shown to my room, where a sliding fusuma door opened to a beautiful space for eating and sleeping. The floor was covered with a tatami mat, and the walls were lined with shoji screens and light wallpaper. Footwear is never worn on tatami, so I took my slippers off before entering the room. A proper tea setting welcomed me.

The meal service, called *washoku*—is a social practice of such significance, it is recognized by the United Nations Educational, Scientific, and Cultural Organization (UNESCO). I sat on a cushion on the floor of my room. Before me was a low table. Being tentative eater, the layout of authentic multi-course dishes was beyond my understanding: there was bowl-after-little-bowl of raw or steamed sauces and sashimis. There were so many things to sample. Even as I was flooded with all those new tastes, I was awestruck by the formality with which every single part of the distinctive tradition is harmoniously prepared. UNESCO says it is associated with an essential spirit of respect for nature that is closely related to the sustainable use of natural resources.

Dinner was followed by a traditional bath called an *onsen*. My private bath was located just outside my room and consisted of a steaming wooden tub. I cautiously dipped the top of a foot in the water, which was so hot

Ryokan attendants

Washoku meal service

it felt like fire. I looked at my foot where it met the simmering water. It turned so red I momentarily thought the skin was gone. I wondered if my hosts were confusing my bath with Japan's annual Walking-over-Fire Festival! It took me forever to get more than my foot into the tub. I tried to enjoy the soak, but my heart was beating faster than I thought it should have. I like a hot bath, but this felt punitive.

Perhaps the temperature was cooling, or maybe I was getting used to it. It occurred to me that maybe I was dying when I finally lowered myself into the scalding water.

When I returned to my room, my table had been reset with evening tea, and my futon was prepared. I eased into the bed and promptly passed out. The next morning the attendant entered the room with breakfast, which, to me, looked very similar to dinner, although I did find an egg.

The ryokan experience serves as a metaphor for why I'm drawn to cultural travel and all the rituals and traditions it offers. Immersing my pedestrian self into new and different worlds continually sharpened my interest in how other people live. The water that day might have been hot, but the experience was so cool.

TURKEY

Lake Wobegon No More

In 1989, after a couple of years working at the U of M, I decided to launch my own independent PR shop. I made the intentional decision to remain a small business with no staff. My new business would not offer large financial rewards, but I did just fine, and most importantly, I had the flexibility to pursue my travel objectives and to shape my journeys to see where they would lead.

One of those early journeys took me to the Middle East, which for years had grabbed my attention and would not let go. So, off I went to Turkey, a great place to begin to explore this ancient and mystifying region.

Turkey's history is alluring, with breathtaking ancient sites from the Sixteen Great Turkish Empires, including the Ottoman Empire, which became one of the most powerful in the world under the reign of Süleyman the Magnificent. Turkey also was my introduction to learning about Islam. Prior to going to Turkey, I had little understanding of Islam. I didn't know about Ramadan or Salat. I didn't understand the significance of the city of Mecca or why Muslims favored a modest dress code.

I arrived quite late at night with no reservations. I was lucky to get a room in a little hotel in the town of Dalyan on Turkey's southwest Mediterranean coast. It was especially dark because there was a power outage. My sparse room didn't have a closet, but with my flashlight, I found lockers. I never stayed in a hotel room with lockers, but since I didn't have anything to hang up, it didn't matter. I had no knowledge of my hotel's surroundings . . . until sunrise.

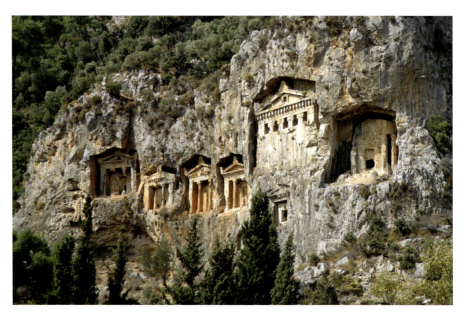

Ancient tombs, Dalyan

One of the Five Pillars of Islam is prayer. I just so happened to be right next to a large mosque, which begins the call to prayer at the first light of day. A *muezzin* (the person who reminds the faithful to come to prayer) cried out. I have since become very familiar with the call to prayer, which is broadcast from a mosque's minarets, but to hear the muezzin for the very first time in my life jolted me out of bed like a rocket. I thought it was some sort of alarm or drill. I've since learned that unless I wish to get up that early in the morning, I'm better served finding a place to stay that is not next door to a mosque.

UNESCO designates places that are considered to be of exceptional value to humanity as natural and cultural heritage sites. When I started to travel internationally in the '60s, I saw many of Europe's most popular World Heritage sites. Witnessing them began to renew my interest in history. I wanted to know who lived in these places, and why and how they built such sites hundreds, if not thousands, of years ago.

UNESCO sites are not just landmark buildings, attractive landscapes, and natural habitats; they are culturally, scientifically, and historically important. They tell us what life was like. Therefore, they take center stage in my itineraries and serve as a backdrop to my stories. Sadly, today, dozens of these sites are threatened by war and conflict, natural disasters, pollution, mass urbanization, and development, and have been moved to the List of World Heritage in Danger. But their significance remains alive and well.

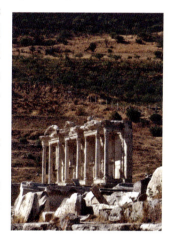

Ephesus

In Turkey, these astonishing heritage sites are found throughout the country. To me, the most impressive Turkish site is Ephesus. In the first century BC, Ephesus had a population of more than 250,000 people. It was the second-largest city in the world and one of the most important commercial and religious centers. Its famous Temple of Artemis is one of the Seven Wonders of the Ancient World.

One of Turkey's other incredible cities is Istanbul, the city of minarets. Istanbul is known for its Ottoman architecture, featuring more than three thousand mosques. I was eager to visit some of the most renowned, including the Hagia Sophia, an architectural masterpiece that was built as a Greek Orthodox Christian Church but has served both Christians and Muslims. Another landmark is the Sultan Ahmed Cami, also called the Blue Mosque because of the exquisite blue tiles on its inside walls. It was designed by Ottoman architect, Mehmed Āghā, to intentionally face Hagia Sophia because Mehmed wanted to show off the Blue Mosque's superior architecture.

Vegetable vendor, Old City of Istanbul

Outdoor café, Istanbul

Hagia Sofia Mosque

I've passed through Turkey several times over the years, and on one of my earliest trips, I made a point of going to a fifteenth-century hammam, one of the oldest and largest authentic Turkish bathhouses in Istanbul. I began the ritual by stripping naked in a "cooling room" before entering the "hot room," a huge, domed, octagonal marble chamber at the center of the hammam. I was seated along a wall where I was instructed to relax and sweat. I was also handed a wooden ladle and told to rinse myself in the nearby basin. Evidently, they wanted to soften me up before they punished me. It was not relaxing, though, to sit stark naked in a bathhouse full of strangers on a hard marble slab for nearly twenty minutes. Each of us was waiting our turn to be slain. At least the sweating part was effortless—it was sweltering in the ornate steam room.

At long last, I was ushered by a strong, sizable attendant to the center of the room where I faced a raised, hot, marble *gobek tasi,* or middle stone, sometimes called a navel stone. The attendant did not speak English, or if she did, she did not seem to be in the mood to chitchat. Let the penance begin.

The attendant, who was topless and once upon a time quite endowed (a visual I will hardly forget), began to scrub me like a washboard with an abrasive mitt lathered in thick suds. Her aim was to exfoliate every dead cell she could possibly find. She trounced and pummeled my defeated body like a piece of meat being tenderized, then hurled me around with her strong, sizable hands until I thought I had taken my last breath. But, no, not yet.

Next came a head massage. And after that thrashing came the last stage of the ordeal, which consisted of her pouring bowls of cold water over my head.

When she was finally done with me, I scurried, humiliated and naked, back to a room where an hour earlier I had timidly undressed and put my clothes in a locker. I was sore. I was exhausted. And I felt great.

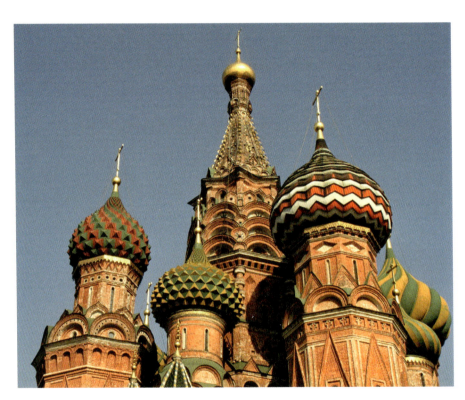
St. Basil's Cathedral

RUSSIA

Jiffy Pop and the KGB

Right after the fall of the Soviet Union in 1991, Harriet, a friend and former airline colleague, formed a company doing business in Russia. It was a popcorn factory, which grew, processed, and sold popcorn and US-made popcorn poppers. Strange as it may sound, she—yes, *she*—built a small manufacturing facility in Krasnodar, on the northeast side of the Black Sea. Harriet was an entrepreneur who worked with local farmers and workers to grow and process hybrid corn into popcorn. She said that in Russia, she was always viewed as an American first, and a woman second. I traveled to Krasnodar to see her operation.

Russia was in a state of economic chaos. The ruble was just about worthless. Most businesses and industries had collapsed, and unemployment was rampant. Even with her many management talents, Harriet had challenges overseeing an operation thousands of miles away. Back then, technology meant undependable faxing rather than the Internet. Communicating during this emerging economy revealed a unique struggle: people had worked for years under the former Soviet state's centralization and were not used to being given responsibility.

One day Harriet heard the popcorn plant was shut down and had been for a couple of weeks. No one had informed her. When, in complete frustration, she asked why, the workers said a part had broken and they weren't sure they should take it upon themselves to do anything about it, to order a new part, or even let their boss know. They had never made those kinds of decisions, as obvious as that one should have been. So, the operation sat idle. Harriet learned the hard way how tough it was to run this otherwise-inventive enterprise with an untested team of enthusiastic, yet inexperienced, partners.

After Krasnodar, I headed north to St. Petersburg on an Aeroflot plane which needed some serious TLC. Greeted by the stench of stale air and a worn and filthy interior, I could hardly lower myself into the seat. I declined all food and beverage. Everyone smoked. But the most memorable part of the flight was the literature that the flight attendant handed out from the little cart she pushed down the aisle. In addition to selling cigarettes and booze, she handed out flyers that made me lean forward in disbelief. I didn't need to read Russian to understand the advertisements, which were clearly peddling products and services for, um, a mature adult audience. These were not your standard duty-free items. The formerly sleepy passengers, most of whom were men, suddenly awoke.

Russia

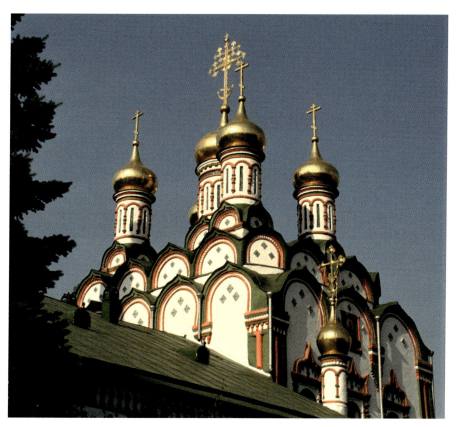

Russian Orthodox onion domes

The airplane could not have landed quickly enough in St. Petersburg. And what a fabulous city St. Petersburg is. Founded in 1703 by Peter the Great, St. Petersburg was, during the Soviet era, renamed Leningrad after Vladimir Lenin, who served as the head of government in the early twentieth century. The city's name reverted to St. Petersburg in 1991 after the fall of the USSR. St. Petersburg is loaded with historic palaces, elaborate museums, and churches with golden, onion-shaped domes. The list of places to see is endless but at the top is its crown jewel, the State Hermitage Museum, the largest art museum in the world. It was founded in 1764 when Catherine the Great acquired a huge collection of paintings and needed a place to hang them. Today, the magnificent museum consists of several buildings, including the Winter Palace, the residence of the Russian emperors for nearly two hundred years.

Hermitage Museum

Church of the Resurrection

Red Square

On an identical plane, I then flew to Moscow, home to yet more outstanding sites, including the Kremlin, Red Square, St. Basil's Cathedral, Lenin's Mausoleum, Bolshoi Theatre, and countless historic and architectural landmarks. Even the stations of the wonderful metro each display their own architecture, featuring colorful arches and ornaments, distinctive brickwork, and carved woodwork.

A shopper seems to be leading the march through Red Square.

I was there just after the fall of the Soviet Union, in the middle of the country's economic breakdown. I witnessed tremendous poverty and despair. In fact, one day, right across the street from the Bolshoi, I saw an older homeless woman collapse and die. A few people came to her side and someone—without urgency—called for an ambulance, which took its sweet time getting there. A couple of medical personnel lifted her into the vehicle, and it slowly drove away. I remember feeling so helpless and sad for her, dying alone on a busy street. I feared what was in store for so many others facing uncertainty and despair.

Homelessness and unemployment increased after the collapse of the Soviet Union.

That same night, I met up with Harriet, whose Russian friends had invited us to their home for a little birthday party . . . for me! Harriet's Moscow administrator was named Sergei. Sergei's father, Mikhail, and his friend, Vladimir, both worked for the KGB before the fall of the USSR. They had helped Harriet retrieve money a Russian man had embezzled from her. Needless to say, the persuasive skills of the KGB had been quite helpful for Harriet. It's who you know.

I wasn't sure what to expect that night, but Mikhail, Vladimir, and their wives could not have been more gracious. In the middle of a devastating economic time, they brought out caviar and vodka and toasted my special day. Being a finicky eater, neither caviar nor vodka-straight-up were the first things I'd order off a menu, but I knew I needed to respect their kindness. So, I threw back the first drink and with my host's insistence, accepted more caviar, followed by another shot of vodka. No, they didn't have to peel the birthday girl off the floor, but during the course of the evening, we had the most insightful conversation.

The former KGB guys talked about how their lives had dramatically changed. They not only lost their jobs but their status; they "lost face," and had no idea what was to come. Furthermore, the country, which had been a world power in government, military, industry, aerospace, and athletics, had fallen hard. In the midst of their grief, my hosts never blinked an eye in welcoming me into their home and treating me to their fineries.

It's been decades since my visit, and Russia has since evolved dramatically by using a methodical misinformation campaign and calculated oppressive strategies to regain its status as a superpower. Today, President Putin's ruthless authoritarian regime has brought terror to Ukraine, panic to its European neighbors, and alarm to the entire world. The results will be tragic. I find myself wondering what parts of the Russian peoples' futures will be taken away as a result of Putin's aggression. Will the rest of the world close their doors to Russia, further impeding the efforts of everyday citizens who are still trying to recover from the fall of the Soviet Union?

What will happen next? There are so many questions . . .

In particular, what roles will the United States, Europe, and China play to calm our fears, restore stability, and attempt to bring peace to a potentially explosive geopolitical landscape? Who will become the next superpowers? And how will they respond to our fragile planet's perilous crises, including war, climate change, humanitarian emergencies, and deteriorating human rights to name a few? What does this changing political climate mean for democracy, freedom . . . and humankind? These are the challenges of our lifetime.

VIETNAM

Following the War of My Generation

As I was finishing high school in 1965, the Vietnam War was intensifying. Many classmates and friends were drafted. Tragically, some died in one of the longest and most controversial wars in American history. More than fifty-eight thousand members of the US armed forces and three million South Vietnamese civilians and soldiers were killed. Another three million were wounded, and twelve million became refugees. The war ended after the withdrawal of US troops in 1973. Vietnam became a unified country in 1976, ruled by North Vietnam. In 1986, the North's communist party elected new leaders who successfully rebuilt trust and put new initiatives in place to turn around the economy. Finally, in 1995, trade with the US was restored, and a new partnership was created.

The following year I went to Vietnam.

I was very concerned about how an American would be greeted. The wounds were still open and raw. Though my visit took place twenty years after the fighting had stopped, I wondered how much animosity I would encounter as a result of America's role in the war. But I found the Vietnamese people to be friendly, welcoming, and universally ready to get on with their lives. When I was there in the mid-'90s, half of the population was under twenty—too young to have known the fighting; and the older folks said they just wanted to move forward. I was not only relieved but taken aback by their genuine friendship toward Americans.

Street vendor

I was traveling with a friend, Nathalia, who had a connection to a family in Hanoi, the thousand-year-old city in northern Vietnam. They ran a modest fruit stand, which they operated from 6:00 a.m. to 10:00

Shave and a haircut

p.m. seven days a week. The couple had two sons, Thang, who was twenty-two, and Loi, who was twenty. Neither could wait to take us around the French-colonial capital on the backs of their motorbikes. *Good Morning, Vietnam*! It was exhilarating, holding on for dear life, taking in the sights, sounds, and smells of Old Hanoi as they weaved in and out of the wild, haphazard traffic. The overwhelming aroma of marinated grilled meats, rice, and vegetables reminded us that everything takes place on the streets: working, cooking, and eating.

Lunchtime in Hanoi

One night, we were treated to dinner at the fruit stand, where we crowded together to enjoy a traditional meal of peanut-sauce marinated chicken wrapped in banana leaves, served, of course, with rice. The dinner was extraordinary, topped only by the generous hospitality of this modest family.

After a few days in Hanoi, we said goodbye to our hosts and headed south along the Red River delta toward Hue in search of a Buddhist temple built into the cliffs of the Huong Tich mountains. We hopped into

Beautiful designs grace ancient palaces.

a small rowboat piloted by a local female farmer. She slowly took us down narrow waterways of the Swallow River, past rice fields and tall grasses on the banks of the flooded valley. The sweltering heat and oppressive humidity drove temperatures over ninety degrees as we hiked up a slippery, rugged path to the temple called the Perfume Pagoda. The temple is located inside the cave and contains statues, shrines, stalagmites, and stalactites, which are said to have their own powers. By this time, in the suffocating heat, I badly needed the deep healing powers this holy cavern promised.

Paddling along the Swallow River

Spiritual Huong Tich cave

Opening My Cultural Lens

The Imperial City of Hue sits on the banks of the Perfume River. Among Hue's many sites is the Thien Mu Pagoda. There is a tale that back in the day if someone was thought to be bad or evil, the offenders were tossed into bronze urns filled with boiling water. I was glad this punishment was no longer practiced but I was on my best behavior just to be sure.

Hue Citadel

Eunuch at Khai Dinh Tomb, Da Nang

South of Hue, along the East Vietnam Sea, is the city of Da Nang, where we visited Khai Dinh's Royal Tomb. It took eleven years to build the tomb, which is the smallest of the other royal tombs constructed during the Nguyen Dynasty. As any good king of his time, he was said to have had thousands of eunuchs and twelve wives, but only one son. Khai Dinh is said to have been particularly close friends with one of his royal guards; rumors abound.

Finally, we arrived in Ho Chi Minh City, formerly Saigon. It was not the dynamic city it is today. Like all of Vietnam at that time, it was just coming out from under punishing reforms. Yet, it was the commercial center of the country and was bustling. Ho Chi Minh City was settled in the seventeenth century by the Khmer, then conquered by the French in 1862. A lot of the architecture, including ornate temples and pagodas, was built under French rule.

Before heading home, we had just a couple more days and decided to take a side trip to Seoul. Our goal was to visit North Korea—the DMZ anyway, as it is the most militarized border on the planet. Since the end of the Korean War, a conflict that claimed three million lives, Korea has been divided geographically, politically, militarily, and ideologically. The demilitarized zone was created in 1953 in the Korean Armistice Agreement and divides South and North Korea in half at this boundary. Regardless of where they live, Koreans are not allowed to cross the border.

Understanding that no one was allowed to visit North Korea, the only way to say, "I've been there" was to go on a South Korean JSA (Joint Security Area) tour, making it possible to cross over that line—in this case, a line on a table—into North Korea.

We took a bus from Seoul through the foothills and arrived about an hour and a half later at the US joint services military base. We stepped off the bus and were led into a mess hall for lunch. I found this strange, but I was hungry and enjoyed the mashed potatoes, gravy, and peas. Then we were informed that jeans were not acceptable attire. It was a fine time to tell us—after we'd arrived. I almost always wear jeans, but on this day, I had on cotton slacks. Nathalia, on the other hand, who rarely wears jeans, decided that day to put them on. We now had a dilemma. A nice young military man, (who I think had an eye for Nathalia), came to our rescue, bringing her a pair of fatigues. It was very thoughtful, though they were ten times too big. The waistband alone was so wide, she had to hold it together with both hands so her pants wouldn't fall down. Nevertheless, we met the dress code.

The time had come to enter North Korea. We were ushered into the famous little blue building in all the DMZ pictures, where we were given a lecture from a US soldier who told us what was about to happen and what not to do. This is an extremely tense border, and following the rules was mandatory. Doing anything stupid might set off a nasty situation. After the military man fully educated us on the history of the Korean War and the establishment of the DMZ, he explained how we were to enter North Korea.

In the middle of the little blue building's conference room was a large rectangular table. Hanging on a long cord from the ceiling, smack dab in the center of the table was a microphone, which monitored everything that was said. We were told to walk, without talking, clockwise around the table. At the halfway point, on the table, floor, and walls was an imaginary demarcation line. We slowly walked around the table, into North Korea, and back again. Mission completed. I had been to North Korea. Little did I know that years later, I would actually spend nearly a week *inside* North Korea.

As I was getting ready to leave the little blue building, however, and go back outside, I fumbled in my coat pocket, trying to find both of my gloves. I could only locate one. Within intentional earshot of the microphone, I whispered to Nathalia, "I think I left one of my gloves in North Korea." Nathalia slapped me upside the head as I endured a sharp glare from one of the soldiers, and a snort and snicker from another. It was clearly time to get on the bus before I created an international incident.

NEPAL

One Foot in Front of the Other

Something I anticipated early in my long arc of traveling was to take on the more physically challenging places first. I knew I would have decades of excursions in front of me, and the older I'd get, the more taxing some of them would become. Oh boy, did that turn out to be true. Trekking and climbing, demanding environments, as well as more adventurous accommodations and food, were considerations I thought about as I planned some of my itineraries. I expected one of those journeys to be Nepal, my first trip to the Himalayas in 1996.

I started out in Kathmandu, Nepal's capital. Nestled in the Himalayan valley, the city is like a living museum, packed with temples and stupas, or dome-shaped Buddhist shrines, including the great stupas of Swayambhunath and Boudhanath. Prayer wheels are a common sight at every temple. Worshipers recite prayers as they turn the wheels clockwise. Colorful prayer flags seen everywhere represent the sky, wind, fire, water, and earth.

Opening My Cultural Lens

Great Stupa of Boudhanath

The Nepalese practice both Buddhism and Hinduism. Unquestionably, the most bewildering experience I had in Kathmandu was witnessing a cremation at the Pashupatinath Temple. The Hindus cremate their dead in very public ceremonies along the river. Family and friends gather around the body as it receives its final rites. The deceased is wrapped in a sheet, and sometimes in an orange satin cloth, and draped with marigolds. At first, I wasn't sure what I was watching. There were lots of people gathering, which always captures my attention. Then I realized I was witnessing a funeral pyre. I was uncomfortable at first, feeling like an intruder. After all, this was someone's funeral and now, their body was burning. Then, as I sat quietly alongside others who were observing the mourners, I, too, became sad. I was awestruck by a ritual I never thought I'd see. It was emotional, but also fascinating.

Nepal

Cremation ceremony, Pashupatinath Temple

After several days in Kathmandu, I flew early in the morning to Lukla, an airstrip carved into the side of a mountain. It sits at nine thousand feet of elevation. The Twin Otter navigated awe-inspiring mountains and landed abruptly, facing uphill, on the short gravel strip. Without taxiing, the airplane quickly spun around so it was in position to take off again from the very top of the runway.

Just like that, I had arrived. My first bit of business was to locate my Sherpa, but after all the other trekkers deplaned and met up with their respective guides, mine was nowhere to be found. I stood by myself next to the plane looking for anyone who appeared to be in search of a single woman traveling alone. I waited there for nearly half an hour, which seemed much longer as my mind raced, and my nervousness escalated. This was my first really big solo trip, and I felt like it was quickly turning into a disaster. I kept thinking about what I'd do if he didn't show up; the airplane hadn't yet left to return to Kathmandu. I then noticed a little building. *Was this the airport's terminal?* I ambled over to the shed just as my Sherpa, Dawa, came out to greet me. His English was marginal, so I didn't know what the miscommunication was, but I was never so happy to see someone in my life. I breathed deeply for the first time in thirty minutes—probably longer, considering we'd landed into the side of the mountain.

Dawa presented me with a walking stick, then introduced me to our short, strong young porter who schlepped my two bags. One contained a week's worth of stuff, and the second was my sleeping bag—a nice warm one I'd been loaned from my pal, Ann Bancroft, an actual Arctic explorer. The porter tossed my stuff on his back and, in flip flops, ran up the mountain trails as if someone had yelled *fire*. In a flash, he was gone. I would not see him again until our day was done. Sherpas, one of the Tibetan ethnic groups that live in the most mountainous regions of the Himalayas, are incredibly hardy fellows.

Porters loaded with heavy bags and gear

Off we went. The transition was so abrupt. One minute I was a stranded, frightened vagabond. The next minute I was off on the trail on a weeklong trek that would take us up to nearly thirteen thousand feet. I didn't have time to think about what just happened because my eyes were suddenly taking in the majestic Himalayas. I would have pinched myself, but I didn't have a free hand.

Khumba Valley

I'd done my homework and fully understood the dangers of high altitudes. I spent weeks back home walking up hills to prepare for the trek and was in good shape, but I could not have trained for this altitude. Dawa made sure I understood how to acclimatize to prevent severe headaches, vomiting, confusion, and worse. On the trails, I saw several rope "ambulance chairs" strapped on the backs of Sherpas who were carrying ailing trekkers back down the mountain. The sick I saw were all younger male hikers who likely thought they were stronger than the altitude. While I was there, a twenty-one-year-old person died.

The first day was the hardest because the altitude hit me like a freight train. This was not a walk in the park. Oxygen was thin. My lungs and muscles needed more. It seemed like every hundred yards I was panting and gasping for air, as my legs struggled to take the next step. I'd have to stop, take in a few deep breaths, and bingo, I'd again be good to go. It took only seconds for the oxygen to return to my lungs and feed my weakened muscles. But the cycle would repeat itself, again and again, all day, every day. Onward we went, working our way up the spectacular Khumbu Valley.

The Himalayas are stunning. Huge snow-covered mountain peaks towered over emerald-green valleys, encircling farms and quaint villages. Along the way, I saw prayer flags sending good wishes through the wind to the heavens, and Buddhist chortens—monuments that protect the area from evil spirits. I needed all the help I could get.

Spiritual chortens

The trails were rugged with jagged rocks. Some were covered with slippery pine needles, and all wore a layer of yak dung. When I'd hear the yak bells coming, I'd immediately find a place to stand to the inside of the trail, against the mountain wall. Never, ever, stand on the outside because yaks are huge and heavy. They lumber along and would knock me over if I'd get in their way. If that would have happened, this would be an obituary. Early on, I got pinned against the wall by a giant yak that forced himself past me, nearly crushing my foot. I was terrified. The beast could have sent me back down the mountain on an ambulance chair, or, I could have gone over the side, arriving down the mountain much faster.

I thought our arrival at the trekker's lodge would never come. I was completely spent. Dawa showed me to my room where, as expected, my bags were waiting. I pulled out my sleeping bag and passed out. Dawa woke me an hour later and insisted I eat some soup. It was going to be a long trek, and I needed nourishment.

The next morning began bright and early. We had to keep moving all the time because it was imperative to get to the next overnight lodge during daylight. My legs felt like they were weighted with lead, and my heart continued to pound. Fatigue sets in quickly. I drank tons of water, but my breaks were limited. I had no choice.

The people who live in the mountains are herders and farmers. They raise yaks for milk, butter, and hides, and grow potatoes and vegetables. The kids were filthy but so darn cute, greeting us with

Dusty young girl seemingly hidden among the rocks

happy shouts of *namaste*. Nepal is one of the poorest countries in the world. The Nepalese life expectancy is under forty years. Until recently, many infants died, and only half of all children reached twenty years of age. People suffer from poor sanitation and all kinds of illnesses and diseases.

Vulnerable children in rural mountain communities

We finally reached Namche Bazaar at 11,286 feet. There we could rest and acclimatize for two nights before continuing. I woke up early the next morning to hike to the top of the town to watch the sunrise over Mt. Everest. I was awestruck, standing in the crisp, cold air beholding Mt. Everest on an ordinary Wednesday on the other side of the globe. At 29,032 feet, it is the tallest peak in the world and nearly three times higher than where I was standing.

Namche Bazaar

In Namche, I took my first "bucket" shower, which had to be done during daylight hours because the temperature at night could get down to twenty degrees. I braced through two showers the entire week, relying on dry shampoo. My hair stood on end, so I just drew my Packers cap down a little further. I looked and smelled like a farm animal. I'm sure I scared the children. The lodges did not have heat or plumbing. There was an occasional generator, but only in the kitchens. I ate porridge for breakfast, and noodle soup for both lunch and dinner.

Nepal

Mt. Everest

I had brought along little packets of instant coffee and hot chocolate. Thank God for my Skippy and trail mix.

The trek continued up to 12,700 feet to Tengboche, the most famous of all of Nepal's monasteries. I went to my first Buddhist ceremony at the temple, taking in the incense, drums, gongs, cymbals, and twenty-foot-long horns called *dungchens*—all part of the daily prayer ceremony. The monks, some of whom were as young as seven when they entered the monastery, chanted and recited scripture during the hypnotic ritual. It was spellbinding! This experience underscored why I was becoming so seduced by cultural travel.

It was time to go back down the mountain to Lukla. Hiking downhill presented its own challenge: tripping. Falling, especially falling forward, could be catastrophic. On the last day, we crossed six long suspension bridges and several other shorter ones, which we never stepped foot on if a yak was coming toward us.

Sherpa

Yaks lumbering across a suspension bridge

As I look back on the trek, after the altitude, the next hardest part was staying mentally engaged. Even in the gorgeous Khumbu Valley, trekking is monotonous. I played every game and sang every song I could to get my mind off the one-step-at-a-time routine. I am clearly not a meditative thinker, yet I was astonished at what the mind—even mine—is capable of. In my mind, I tried to recreate my grandmother's Thanksgiving dinner. For hours and hours, I focused on walking in her front door and being met by the savory scents of turkey, mashed and sweet potatoes, gravy, stuffing, squash, and green bean casserole, followed by pumpkin and sweet mincemeat pies. Grandma always kept a list of what was on her menu and the list always began with a relish tray and concluded with nuts and mints. She was a traditionalist, and sitting at her table was an honor. In its mysterious way, my mind drifted to the aroma of that room. I swear on her grave, not only could I smell it, but I could taste it, too.

At the end of the trek, I felt like I was a soldier coming home from the battleground. I was hungry and dirty, and so relieved it was over. But it was worth it! I crawled into Lukla, expressed my gratitude to Dawa, then hopped on the Twin Otter with several other trekkers who looked and stunk as bad as me. The anticipation of a shower and a real dinner was overpowering. But we had to get off the ground first—a white-knuckle event. The pilot revved up the plane's engines to a roaring full steam, released the brakes, and blasted down the steep, carved runway to get enough oomph to lift off and then up, attempting to clear mountainsides so close I felt I could have touched them. The pilot had one and only one shot. What a rush! The only thing that topped it was my exceptionally long, hot shower in Kathmandu and the proper meal that followed. The glass of wine wasn't bad either.

Shopping at the Písac market, Sacred Valley of the Incas

PERU & GALÁPAGOS

Inca Dinka Do

Like so many people, I had Machu Picchu on my bucket list. While I knew the hiking would not compare to Nepal, the altitude at the top of the fifteenth-century citadel was not to be taken for granted. In 1997, I flew from Lima to Cuzco to acclimate before continuing on to Machu Picchu and the Sacred Valley of the Incas. Cuzco's altitude, while higher than Machu Picchu, is about eleven thousand feet. To avoid sickness, I was advised to just relax and not do much for a day.

Having just trekked in Nepal, I opted out of the four-day hike from Cuzco. Instead, I took a train to Aguascalientes, which sits at the foot of Machu Picchu. The scenic ride runs through the Sacred Valley alongside the rapid, rocky Urubamba River and its rugged canyon. I stayed at a small hotel and began my hike up the mountain the following morning.

Opening My Cultural Lens

Quechua teen, Cuzco valley

Vendor, Aguascalientes

Machu Picchu is the remains of an entire Inca community that sits on top of a remote mountain. It is invisible until you reach the peak; a very clever protection against invaders. It was abandoned when the Spanish began their conquest in the 1530s. Because of its hidden location, it wasn't discovered until 1911.

Machu Picchu

While no one is certain why it was built and exactly who lived there, the citadel's ruins represent one of the most significant cultural, religious, and political centers of the Inca Empire. A World Heritage site, it was constructed without mortar, yet its huge stone blocks are set so tightly together even a piece of paper can't fit between them. I continued to wonder how in the world these workers got these huge stones up the mountain without the use of wheels.

Machu Picchu is known for its astronomical alignments. One of the best examples and most sacred sites is the Sun Temple. The temple's window is perfectly positioned to capture sunlight during Southern Hemisphere's winter solstice on June 21. Machu Picchu is an example of ingenious engineering with its irrigation systems and six hundred terraces, which were built to prevent the ruins from sliding down the mountain.

Being so close to the Galápagos Islands, I extended my trip to include a week on another kind of safari: observing wildlife found nowhere else in the world. I needed to first get back to Cuzco, then fly to Lima to transfer to Quito, where my cruise was to depart the next day. It was a good plan, until I got sick. I learned the hard way: never, ever eat anything that hasn't been cooked, or that has been peeled.

Overlooking Machu Picchu's steep hillsides

By the time I got to Lima, I had experienced all the effects one might imagine from food poisoning and fever. I was in a bad way. At the Lima airport, I couldn't wait for the flight to board so I could sleep, but I had no such luck. The flight was delayed by an hour, then another hour—making it nearly four hours total before taking off. I had more problems on what should have been a two-plus-hour flight to Quito. The city's location on the equatorial line in the mountains and some approaching storms added up to a bad situation. We circled and circled. I had the chills, then the sweats, and felt like I was going to faint. I no sooner drained my bottle of water when I needed a refill. The flight attendant, who was not enjoying this leg of her trip either, was not very accommodating. I was on my own.

After another hour of circling, we were informed that we needed to refuel and would be heading to Cali, Columbia, home to one of the most notorious drug cartels in the world. Traveling in and out of drug-trafficking hot spots in Latin America makes customs and immigration officials very thorough. I know this because I had been strip-searched on a prior trip while leaving Rio de Janeiro. Could this trip get any longer?

Because it was now 9:00 p.m., the Cali airport was closed. There was no one at customs to process a plane full of passengers. We waited. By now, I was so weak that I was slow in dragging myself off the plane, only to wind up at the end of the long line. When I finally got to a motel, it was 3:00 a.m. I got about an hour of sleep. We were to return to the airport bright and early to catch a 7:00 a.m. flight back to Quito.

Because of the long delay, I missed my ship to the Galápagos. I couldn't get on another until the following day, which was a blessing in disguise because I was still sick and worn out. Since I now had a day in Quito, I had one errand to run: find a doctor. I walked to a clinic and asked for *el médico*. My Spanish is pitiful at best, and all I could mutter was, "*Tengo amebas.*" *El médico* broke into a big smile. (Why he smiled, I'm not sure.) "*Ah! Sí, amebas!*" he said as he gave me some serious meds. Let the healing begin.

My flight to the Galápagos landed in San Cristóbal, where I boarded the small ship that introduced me to birds and animal species that are unique to the islands. When I was there, travelers were required to sleep overnight on their ships. The government of Ecuador also limited the number of ships, and hence, the number of visitors, to the fragile islands. My intimate ship had only six other passengers, plus the crew, which included a wildlife specialist with scientific expertise.

Intriguing wildlife species

Located six hundred miles off the coast of Ecuador, this archipelago of thirteen main volcanic islands is so extraordinary that it inspired Charles Darwin's *On the Origin of Species*, which described his theory of evolution by natural selection. The Galápagos has more than four hundred species of fish, twenty-three species of reptiles, fifty-six native bird species, and twenty-nine migrant species. We'd island-hop day after day to explore the habitat of an array of wildlife endemic to the islands, including marine iguana; the giant Galápagos tortoise, which can weigh more than nine hundred pounds; flightless cormorants; and the Galápagos penguin, the only penguin species in the Northern Hemisphere. While there, I even had the chance to snorkel with sea lions.

Marine iguana

Giant tortoise

These birds and animals are completely protected and therefore have no fears of humans. There are strict policies in place to ensure travelers don't touch the wildlife. Even so, as a photographer, I had the ability to get up close and personal. I carefully crawled to within inches of the creatures—even birds resting on their eggs or tiny babies.

PAPUA NEW GUINEA

Some Things I Can't Tell My Mother

The more I traveled, the more intrigued I became with cultures and environments that are at risk of dramatic change because of modernization. So, in addition to going to places that would require considerable physical stamina, I also felt an urgency to visit places whose cultures are disappearing. A friend had done extensive work as a broadcast journalist for a Twin Cities TV station that had a commitment to global news. The station sent Colleen to cover news in several international locations, including to live for three weeks with a New Guinea headhunting tribe called the Asmat. I was mesmerized with her out-of-this-world stories and knew my next trip, in 1998, would explore some of these fascinating places.

Located in the Pacific Ocean, northeast of Australia, New Guinea is home to a few tribal cultures that continue to maintain a subsistence lifestyle, utilizing natural resources for their livelihoods. In addition to Tok Pisin, a whopping 836 distinct languages are spoken.

The country is divided into Irian Jaya to the west and Papua New Guinea to the east. I was headed to Papua New Guinea.

While Papua New Guinea's urban areas are changing rapidly, the villages are holding on to their simple lifestyle, and the deeper into the jungle I went, the less had changed. Getting around parts of the country could only be done by air. I hopped on a little prop—one of five such flights I chartered while there—to reach the impenetrable rainforest of the eastern highlands.

Asaro Mudmen

We began with a hike through the jungle to see the Asaro Mudmen, a group that performs a dance commemorating a famous battle between two villages many years ago. My guide, Kaut, translated the legend: the men from Asaro were not very good warriors, and during one battle, they fled across a river only to end up covered with thick, grey mud. They took one look at each other and became startled.

Then they wondered if their shocking appearance would have the same effect on their enemies. So, the next morning, the clever mud warriors crept up on the enemy village. The women from the other tribe began screaming that the "evil spirits of the water" were coming. The enemy, which wasn't so brave after all, became scared and fled. Then the Asaro warriors persuaded the women from the other tribe to return with them to their village, which they did. And so, the Mudmen prevailed and won the girls too. To this day, the village elders keep the tale alive.

While Kaut was recounting all of this, I noticed a group of women who were beginning to dress in special clothing, placing feathers one by one into their headdresses, preparing for a Sing-Sing, a very traditional ceremony. The brilliant costumes and headdresses, many of them handed down through the generations, are made up of grasses and feathers, including those of the bird of paradise. While the women were off in one corner, the men were putting on full battle dress. The participants spent more than two and a half hours preparing their costumes.

Then, to the surprise of my guide, they performed the three parts of a Sing-Sing. Kaut explained how rare this was because it is never done informally.

Colorful face paintings at a Sing-Sing

Sing-Sing celebrations, which happen throughout the year and can last for days, bring together other villages to share their respective, colorful traditions. The dancers and singers lined up and moved in unison while chanting and singing ancient songs. The first part is performed by the girls, the second part by the boys, and in the third part, they dance together. These folks take their traditions and spirits very seriously, and their dancing is proud and fierce.

Afterward, the chief gathered everyone around and said he was impressed by my interest and hoped that I would take back good memories to America. But their hospitality was not finished. The chief insisted on showing me the rest of his village.

Among the things he wanted me to see was a skull house where skulls of several of the village elders—and members of his own family, such as his father—rest. Cannibalism and head-hunting were practiced until the '50s. Kaut informed me. He said the head was sometimes not eaten, but it was hung in the doorway of the spirit house. Evidently, that was good for me to know. Without Kaut, I followed the chief on a narrow path into the jungle toward the skull

On the way to the skull house

Meet dad.

house, which was pretty creepy, but obviously very important to the chief. I walked behind him. He wore nothing but a loincloth. *There are some things I just can't tell my mother*, I kept thinking. And there they were. A room full of skulls. I was introduced to all of them.

My next flight took us farther north to Karawari. We landed less than a hundred yards from a river and were met by a bunch of young kids who took us to a small boat. Each day we'd travel down the river and through smaller waterways to access even more remote areas. Then, we'd hike through dense jungle to villages infrequently visited by any outsiders.

In one of these villages, I sat with some kids who wanted to hold my hand and touch my arms. Kaut said these kids had never seen a white person before.

Later, the same kids and a couple of their mothers thought it would be fun to teach me how to dance. I'm not above looking foolish, and my lack of skill seemed to be enjoyed by all. Still, my "creative" dance moves were rewarded afterward when some of the women cooked up some treats for me to enjoy. It was a sweet gesture—except they were assorted little reptiles, roasted over an open fire. *The more burned, the better*, I thought. I wanted to wash them down with a cold beer, but there is no such luck in the jungle.

Kaut lived in the Karawari region, which has more than two hundred recorded languages, hundreds of endemic birds, thousands of native plants, and four thousand species of orchids.

Here in Karawari, as well as most parts of remote Papua New Guinea, everything runs on generators, and these shut down at nightfall. There is no phone, only a short-wave radio. Accommodations were basic.

Kaut told me clans today continue to fight over women, land, and pigs. Pigs are a significant asset because they retain their value, signify a person's wealth, and can be an important part of a bride's price.

Opening My Cultural Lens

People here are very loyal, and when invited to something, they show up or have a darn good excuse not to, because people here also retaliate. If someone is offensive, they may be cut off from the socialization of the village, including the food sharing, which can be devastating. Kaut said if someone has done something really bad, they might find their head on a stick. Good to know.

When a girl begins womanhood, she has marks cut into her back during initiation rites; when a young man reaches puberty, they cut his penis up the side. In some areas, they cut into the boys' backs, producing raised scars representing crocodile skin. Then, they all dance and eat a pig.

Siblings, Karawari

Initiation scars

In Madang, on the northern coast, everyone, even the boys and girls, were chewing betel nut, which they shimmied up trees to collect. First, you chew the nut to soften it. Then, you dip some mustard into a little lime and mix it with the nut in your mouth. It turns red, involves a lot of spitting, and gives you a little buzz. Eventually, your teeth rot and fall out, a side effect no one seemed to mind.

Sorcery is very important in this culture. Tattoo, a witch doctor I was introduced to, said natural herbal medicines are common and can cure most ailments. People look to native plants to heal pain, fever, snake bites… you name it.

Papua New Guinea

Tatoo, the witch doctor   Girl wearing traditional bilas

Costumes are adorned with ceremonial accents such as large crescent-shaped kina shells, pig tusks, and dog's teeth. These accents are called *bilas.* They are very valuable because they are often passed down from prior generations. "If someone intentionally destroys a bila, they could be killed," Kaut told me.

People make masks and other art to represent their respective tribes in ceremonies. They're carved from soft wood and decorated with shells, feathers, human hair, and pig tusks. Some masks represent power, while others honor ancestors, fend off evil spirits, or are used in hunting. I bought some of the exotic masks, carvings, and a penis gourd, called a *koteka.* It's authentic. Look it up. Tied around their waists, a koteka is decorated with twine and shells and traditionally is worn by men in some areas of the highlands to cover their, well, you know. Some men only wear a koteka during ceremonies,

Opening My Cultural Lens

but others wear it daily as a main piece of their clothing, which I'm told also can functionally be used as a sort of a handy little purse.

We flew to the southern highlands, home to the Huli Wigmen. They are the largest ethnic tribe in this area, and they have one of the most colorful traditions. We traveled to a village where one of the Wigmen, named Willy, came to meet me and show me the elaborate face paint of their Sing-Sing. The Wigmen are known for their intricately decorated wigs made from human hair, which is usually their own but can be donated by their wife and children. After Willy completed his wig, he began the long process of meticulously applying face paint. Children sat around him, watching Willy's every move because they knew they would one day perform in a Sing-Sing. After Willy colored his beard and eyes, he applied yellow paint on his face, the entire process taking two hours.

Teaching the next generation how to prepare for a Sing-Sing

Papua New Guinea

Finishing touches of ceremonial face paint

At the end of each day on every trip, I journal. If I don't take thorough notes during the day, turn them into pages at night and confirm my recollections with my guides the next day, I simply could never document details I can't risk forgetting. Papua New Guinea tested my ritual. There was so much I learned. I could ill afford to miss a single experience.

Prayer flags

BHUTAN

I Thought I Could Be a Buddhist

Shangri-la is described as a remote utopia, a mystical and harmonious paradise where life approaches perfection. It's supposed to be imaginary.

I've been to Shangri-la.

Never had I experienced a culture centered on joy and peace—that is until I visited Bhutan, a world so fundamentally influenced by Buddhism that it stands apart from any other place on Earth.

I first became acquainted with Buddhism, one of the major religions practiced in the Himalayas, on my Nepal trek. I was intrigued with its colorful rituals, its prayer flags, prayer wheels, *chortens,* and *stupas.* But it wasn't until I went to Bhutan in the late '90s that I witnessed the philosophy of Buddhism. Bhutan bowled me over.

Located on the eastern side of the Himalayas, surrounded by China and India, this small country is one of the most unique places on the planet. The government mandates that the preservation of Bhutan's environment and culture comes before economic development. Well, there's a thought.

Simple farms dot the foothills.

I understand a lot has changed in the kingdom since I was there. In those days, there was no Internet or social media—indeed, there was little that connected the Bhutanese to the outside world. There also was virtually no pollution, litter, crime, or political problems. Everyone had work and a home, was ruled by a beloved king, and seemed happy.

In fact, whereas almost every other country in the world measures its wellbeing according to an economic index (the gross domestic product or GDP), Bhutan measures wellbeing according to GNH—gross national happiness. Say what? This remarkable philosophy of quantifying happiness on measures other than economics guides its people and government alike. Accordingly, the Bhutanese are universally compassionate, respectful, and kind. All the time. Their dispositions are peaceful and relaxed—completely unruffled.

Ruled by King Jigme Khesar Namgyel Wangchuck, a fifth-generation *Druk gyalpo,* or dragon king, Bhutan is fiercely independent and self-sufficient. When I went, the country restricted the number of visitors, charged each a hefty per diem, and assigned each a government-issued guide.

A young monk radiates peace and compassion.

My guide's name was Karma. How perfect. Being with Karma was like taking a master class. He wanted to show me why Bhutan was special and sacred. Most

Bhutanese practice a similar sect of Buddhism as Tibet and believe the Dalai Lama is the reincarnation of the Buddha of Compassion, so it's no wonder that compassion guides its history, politics, and culture.

I figured early on that while I revere Buddhist philosophy, I was not a good candidate to actually become a Buddhist. I'm not that introspective, and I don't have the patience to meditate. Though the Dalai Lama says when we practice compassion, the heart of Buddhism, we have more strength, peace, and joy. If you want others to be happy, practice compassion. If you want to be happy, practice compassion. Simple and profound.

Turning the prayer wheel accumulates good karma.

Bhutan is divided into state-like districts, each with an architecturally distinctive *dzong*, a fortress-monastery that serves as the seat of civil and religious power and also houses monks. I visited numerous dzongs, including one in Jakar, where we stumbled upon a village festival. It featured a lively, masked dance in which drums and gongs were used to cast away evil spirits. The dance I saw celebrated the arrival of Guru Rinpoche on a snow lion to introduce Buddhism and proclaim the elimination of evil. Mask festivals are very common, and while they are fun, the rituals are taken seriously.

We hiked a lot at high altitudes, taking in the cold, clean air. Prayer flags waved over the countryside, and prayer wheels were turned by worshippers to get rid of negative karma—or so explained Karma. Inside each prayer wheel were copies of mantras that spin to multiply the number of prayers.

Trongsa Dzong

Along my journey, I had the honor of being blessed by monks several times. I would bow with folded hands as they touched my head and chanted blessings to rid me of bad karma. Then the monks would place a white silk prayer scarf around my neck, symbolizing purity and compassion.

Compassion is ever-present for all things big and small. One day, Karma and I were walking around the grounds of a temple when a mosquito landed on his arm. He gently waved the little creature away. *Hmm*, I thought to myself, *I wonder how compassionate I will be back home during the summertime dusk.* One more reason I couldn't become a Buddhist.

Probably one of the most unexpected treats was being invited to observe a performance by Bhutan's Royal Academy of Performing Arts. Maybe it was just a rehearsal, as I was the only one in the audience. It's considered a very auspicious and spiritual exercise to witness sacred mask dances, which are also important social events. The outdoor courtyard ceremony featured a series of eight different mythological mask dances, all representing how the evil spirits are subdued.

Royal Bhutan Academy of Performing Arts

A single rough primary road connects one side of the mountainous country to the other, and the drive becomes scarier as elevation increases. The road twists with terrifying hairpin turns. The mountainside drops away from the road nearly vertically, and so each twist offers a view down—straight down—to what would be a quick and certain death. I had to close my eyes. My driver, Wangdi, never got the Land Rover out of second gear as we meandered past stunning valleys, farms, and miles of protected forests that are home to spectacular birds and animals.

Bashful boy, Wangdue Phodrang

I've always been well cared for by guides, drivers, pilots—and even a few headhunters. All have been protective and wise. I've trusted them with my life, literally, everywhere I travel. Yes, many treacherous roads have scared the bejesus out of me. Sure, I'd just about lose my lunch when trying to land on a mountain or jungle airstrip, places where do-overs are not an option. Of course, I feel apprehension and anxiety—though never fear. I honestly believe that some of life's events are fate—what will happen will happen.

Perhaps I visited Bhutan when it was indeed a Shangri-la. All I know is that I happened upon a mystical place founded on Buddhist principles. These are practiced through meditation and prayer and are ultimately intended to nourish happiness and enlightenment. It's an idyllic paradise that I didn't think could exist on this imperfect planet, a one-of-a-kind place that puts its environment and its culture before economic development.

What a shock it was this time to return to the United States. Going through customs and then the terminal, I was acutely aware of people around me who were arguing, behaving rudely to others, scolding their children, and walking around with facial expressions and body language that expressed impatience and anxiety. Welcome home.

The Himalayas

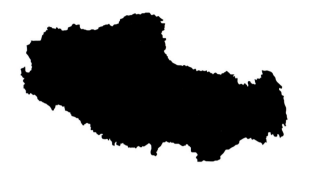

TIBET

Rooftop of the World

To me, one of the most visually powerful and dramatic places on the planet is the Himalayas. There's just something about these endless jagged, snow-capped peaks and gorges. They are hypnotic yet peaceful. After seeing the world's tallest mountains in Nepal and Bhutan, I wanted to return, this time to Tibet.

For hundreds of years, Tibet was the most devout Buddhist nation in the world. But in 1950, this tranquil country became a strategic acquisition for the Chinese. China's new communist regime insisted that Tibet's liberation was best for the Tibetans because, China said, both countries would be stronger as one.

The 14th Dalai Lama was only fifteen years old in 1950 when thirty-thousand Chinese soldiers attacked Lhasa, Tibet's capital. The Tibetans didn't stand a chance. After years of turmoil, the Dalai Lama, at the ripe age of twenty-one, went to Beijing to meet with Chairman Mao Zedong. Mao cunningly led the Dalai Lama to believe that

Tibet's political system and Tibetan Buddhism would be protected if Tibet recognized China's rule. That didn't work out so well. The hostility continued.

In 1959, as crowds in Lhasa prepared to celebrate the Tibetan New Year, word spread that the Chinese planned to kidnap or kill the Dalai Lama. The ensuing violence left fifteen thousand Tibetans dead. Disguised as a Chinese soldier, the Dalai Lama escaped over the Himalayas to Dharamshala, India, where he lives in exile today.

Sadly, this enchanting land has changed, maybe forever. Condemned by the United Nations, the Chinese "liberation" killed 1.2 million Tibetans and drove one hundred thousand into exile. The Chinese Red Guards set out to abolish the Four Olds: old thinking, old cultures, old habits, and old customs. Thousands of monasteries and shrines were destroyed, and natural resources and wildlife were devastated. Farmers were told what to grow and when to grow it. Anyone resisting was beaten or jailed. Today, the Chinese monitor everything Tibetans do, making them paranoid and afraid.

Tibet's monasteries hold a significant cultural and spiritual place in the hearts of its people. Though many were shut down or destroyed by the Chinese, several still serve a central role in all aspects of Tibetan life. The Jokhang Monastery, a World Heritage site, was founded as the religious and geographical center of Lhasa.

Among the largest and most famous of the remaining monasteries is Potala Palace. It used to be the government center and residence of the Dalai Lama. Atop a hill overlooking Lhasa, it is a place of spiritual pilgrimage, boasting more than one thousand rooms, ten thousand shrines, and two hundred thousand statues.

Potala Palace

In Buddhism, there are many kinds of *lamas* who are important figures, if not founders, of monasteries. The higher-status lamas are believed to be reincarnated. Among them is the Panchen Lama, who is the second greatest spiritual leader of Tibet. Two weeks after the last Panchen Lama died in 1989, the current one was chosen. The process requires young monks to be presented to the Dalai Lama. He then meditates and visualizes the Panchen Lama's reincarnation. Based on those visualizations, he chooses the new Panchen Lama. Likewise, the Panchen Lama chooses the next Dalai Lama. The Tibetans believe the Dalai Lamas are the manifestations of the Buddha of Compassion and are reincarnated for the purpose of serving other human beings.

Woman praying at a monastery

The current Panchen Lama was only six years old in 1995 when he and his parents were captured by the Chinese. The world's youngest political prisoner has not been seen or heard from since. Conveniently, the Chinese took it upon themselves to select their own Panchen Lama, who just happens to be the son of a communist party member. And that's not all: the Chinese believe their Panchen Lama will identify the next Dalai Lama, ultimately taking away this spiritual decision from the Tibetan Buddhists and letting the communist Chinese decide who the next Dalai Lama will be.

Opening My Cultural Lens

Eclectic styles posing for a class picture

Preparing for monkhood

The Chinese also are known to bug the monasteries and even to dress undercover as monks. My guide said most of the new jobs are going to the Chinese who are moving into the area. Tragically, many describe what is happening to Tibet as cultural cleansing.

North of Lhasa, at an altitude of nearly thirteen thousand feet, is Ganden, one of the "great three" monasteries. A long and winding road with dramatic views of the surrounding valleys leads to the fifteenth-century monastery atop Wangbori Mountain. The giant complex comprises more than fifty buildings that reflect traditional Tibetan Buddhist monastery architecture. *Ganden* means joyous. Ironically, Ganden suffered most at the hands of the Chinese Red

Chortens house sacred Buddhist relics.

Ganden Monastery

Guards, probably because of its political influence at the time. Before the Chinese takeover, more than two thousand monks lived there; today, there are four hundred.

Tibet and Bhutan are home to a similar sect of Buddhism, and I had expected my visit to Tibet to leave me with the same sense of peace and contentment I felt in Bhutan. But it was not so; instead, I felt a deep sadness. This once-magical kingdom, governed by love and compassion, has been nearly stripped of its rich culture and religion. What is left, instead, is a tourist attraction.

Don't count the Tibetans out, however. They are proud, tenacious, and determined to share their story with activists around the world who have been inspired to help Tibet rebuild its incredible culture and preserve its heritage. That gives me hope and joy.

Life in the high altitudes

CHINA

Before Gucci Gotcha

From Tibet, I flew over those drop-dead gorgeous Himalayas to mainland China. I first visited China in the late '80s, when it was remarkably different from today: buildings in Beijing were only a few stories tall, no English was spoken, all signage was in Mandarin, and everyone rode bikes, so there was no smog. But modernization came lightning fast to a country that had just ended the Cultural Revolution. Overnight, China transformed its economy. When I went back to Beijing less than ten years later, it was unrecognizable—it was like traveling in a time machine. Skyscrapers and highways ringed the city, and the retail landscape centered on luxury brands such as Gucci, Cartier, and Rolex. Airports as big as LAX served cities I had never heard of yet were home to millions.

Bicycles were the main mode of transportation in the '80s.

The Great Wall

But China's development has come at an environmental cost. I recall hiking at the Great Wall more than thirty years ago when the air was clean and clear. When I returned just a few years later, yellow smog blanketed Beijing and the famous site. The previously amazing Great Wall was sorrowfully forgettable.

On this trip in 2003, I was really jazzed to visit Yunnan Province in southwestern China. Yunnan is home to twenty-five of China's fifty-nine ethnic nationalities. UNESCO recognizes this region for its extraordinarily colorful mix of traditions, customs, and languages.

Kindergarten can combine child care and education.

Yunnan's fusion of cultures includes the Han, China's dominant ethnic group. While Mandarin is China's national tongue, most minorities also speak their own languages. An outsider can only tell these groups apart by their colorful attire, which meant for great photography.

Afternoon card game

China has been influenced by Taoism, Confucianism, and Buddhism, sometimes entwined with animism, another ancient belief. Confucianism is a philosophy that defines codes of conduct and patterns of obedience. Taoism is more of a philosophy of mystical insight, living in harmony with the universe. Buddhists believe that all life is suffering, due to desire, and that happiness can only be achieved if desire is overcome. There is a saying in China that many Chinese are Confucianists for most of their lives, Taoists in retirement, and Buddhists before death. During the Cultural Revolution, religion was denounced by the communists as superstition. As a result, many Chinese are atheists.

Taoism teaches how to balance one's life.

Opening My Cultural Lens

Burning incense at temple, Dali

Jack, my young guide, was a delight to travel with and told me he was inspired by my escapades as a solo cultural traveler and hoped he could do the same one day. (I think he had a cute admiration-based crush on me.) We began in the three-thousand-year-old city of Dali, the province's first settlement. We walked throughout its eclectic neighborhoods, chatting with people and learning about their customs. We went to the top of the 13,500-foot-high Cangshan Mountain, where there is a Taoist temple. The Taoists believe in heaven rather than reincarnation, and so they burn yellow scriptures as incense to carry their prayers to heaven in the smoke. I lit and placed some paper incense in a burner and knelt as a priest blessed me. He gave me a jade laughing-Buddha necklace that I was to wear close to my heart for good luck.

A ten-hour drive northwest brought us to Lijiang, home to the Bai ethnic group. Bai means white in Chinese, and it is the predominant color of the ethnic

Bai headdress, Lijiang

group's traditional dress. Like all the various groups, Bai girls wear distinctive clothing and headdresses representing the moon, wind, flowers, and snow. They cut the white tail off their headdress when they become engaged or married.

The different ethnic groups that live in the region don't always get along. At the Sunday market in the small town of Niujie, we found a group called the Yi, a clan society whose elders remain

Bai architecture, Xizhou

Opening My Cultural Lens

in charge of the social order. The Yi fiercely resisted the Han. Chairman Mao Zedong called the Han barbarians.

Among another ethnic group, the Naxi, women work in the fields, raise the children, cook, and clean while the men play cards and listen to music. Men are the heads of the household and are said to be artistic: writers, poets, and musicians.

Naxi's Dongba faith practices living in harmony with nature.

Contrarily, the Mosuo, who call themselves Na, are matriarchal. They maintain flexible arrangements for their love affairs. There are no Mosuo words for marriage, virginity, husband, or wife. A couple can become lovers without setting up joint residency. A man spends the night at a woman's house but returns at dawn to his mother's house to live and work.

Any children born to the couple grow up in the mother's family, raised by the women. The father provides support. The women inherit the property, and disputes are overseen by female elders. This social system was banned in the Cultural Revolution when monogamy became required. Even so, elements of this lifestyle still exist today.

Progressive Mosou women hold the power.

Jack and I had to part in Yunnan, but he had a special gift for me before we said goodbye. He is originally from this area in China, and his mother still lives nearby. When Jack and I first arrived, he had shared with his mom how interested I was in Chinese traditions. While we were out gallivanting one day, his mother made me a beautiful jade bracelet to symbolize good luck. To this day, I wear it all the time, verklempt for this meaningful remembrance.

After a long goodbye, I made my way southeast to Guilin, one of the most majestic UNESCO Natural Heritage sites in the world. Clusters of limestone peaks were created millions of years ago when India collided with Asia to form the Himalayas. The mountains that surround the Lijiang (or Li) River are known for their sheer vertical surfaces, caves, sinkholes, and underground streams.

Limestone mountains, Guilin

One day on the tranquil river, I went fishing with a guy who still practices the age-old art of using trained cormorants to fish. No pole or bait, just a boat full of as many as a dozen birds. The fisherman ties a string around a bird's throat to prevent it from swallowing the fish. The cormorants are turned loose to dive and catch larger fish. Smaller fish can squeeze through, so at least the cormorant gets an hors d'oeuvre. The cormorant returns to the boat, where the fisherman squeezes its neck below its beak so it coughs up the fish, which flies out into a pail. It's the strangest sight. Some birds catch as many as five large fish at once, all stuck in their throat. Cormorants live to be twenty years old and will fish with the same fisherman throughout their life—and probably the fisherman's, too.

Fishing with cormorants, Li River

This trip would not be complete without going to Chengdu. And, oh, what a treat was in store. I was about to visit a sanctuary dedicated to the protection and breeding of giant pandas, which are widely recognized as a national treasure. I was accompanied by two Chinese guides at the Chengdu Research Base of Giant Panda Breeding, located in Sichuan Province in western China. At the time, it housed about forty pandas.

It was late in the day and raining, so there were no other visitors there. My agent had arranged for me to meet with a scientist to learn more about the creatures' habits and breeding. The scientist asked if I'd like to hold a cub. I couldn't believe it! A crew dressed me in a sterile gown, boots, and gloves. I looked like I was about to go into surgery.

The scientist came out carrying a big ball of fur named Cheng Gong. He was just under a year old and weighed about seventy pounds. He was determined to scratch an itch and kept sliding around, nearly falling out of my arms, but I held on as long as I could,

Pandas are vulnerable because their habitat is threatened.

enjoying the moment. Holding him was one of the most awesome experiences I've ever had.

There are fewer than two thousand pandas left in the world. One of the reasons they're so threatened is because they're very finicky eaters. They have huge appetites, but most of their diet is a certain species of bamboo.

To make matters worse, they're just not very interested in mating. Pandas are solitary animals, so even if they want to mate, just finding another panda can be a challenge. They're also fussy about who they mate with. To make mating even more difficult, female pandas are in heat for less than seventy-two hours per year.

It seems it's not enough to just put a couple of cute pandas in the same room for a while. Scientists have had to use unorthodox measures to move the process along. Some male pandas are known to have been given a little boost, like Viagra, to put them in the mood. Others are actually shown videos of other pandas mating—that's right, panda porn—hoping they may become inspired.

If all that is successful, then comes birthing. Most new, inexperienced mothers—animals or otherwise—instinctively know how to deliver a baby. Not so with pandas. Nearly 60 percent of new cubs die shortly after birth. I watched a film about a panda giving birth. After the mother delivered and dropped the cub, she slapped the poor infant around on the ground like it was a toy. She wasn't trying to hurt it; she was just playing. The scientists had to carefully get the cub out of harm's way, and then get themselves out of the way of the mother.

After a bazillion hours of controlled research, some experts think it may be as simple as this: if a couple of pandas are lucky enough to hit it off and are meant for each other, babies might follow. In the meantime, the giant pandas remain endangered.

Excavator

EGYPT

How'd You Get So Funky?

My rising interest in history was not only informing my photography but taking center stage in better understanding the context of each destination. So, it was no surprise that the next stop listed on the board was Egypt, which has not just protected its heritage sites but continues to unearth more remarkable treasures every year. One piece at a time, archaeologists are uncovering the lives of people who formed civilizations thousands of years ago.

For example, one of the most famous discoveries was made by two British archaeologists who found the three-thousand-year-old gold coffin, which contained the mummified remains of the teenaged King, Tutankha-

Ready for delivery

mun. More recently, in 1995, an American archaeologist discovered the burial place of dozens of the sons of Ramses II, who—quite the stud himself—had more than one hundred kids, including fifty-two sons. In 2021, in Luxor, Aten—the 3,400-year-old "lost golden city"—was discovered. It is the largest ancient city ever uncovered in Egypt and the biggest discovery since Tutankhamun's tomb.

Egyptian pharaohs ruled as early as five thousand years ago, building massive monuments such as the Great Pyramids of Giza—the planet's oldest manmade attraction and one of the Seven Wonders of the Ancient World. The Pyramids had been around for 2,500 years by the time Christ was born. Historians still don't know exactly why or how they were built; they know there are tombs inside, but they aren't sure that was the Pyramids' only purpose.

The pharaohs believed in eternal life, which is why their tombs contained treasures they wanted to take with them after they died. The burial sites contain mummies, hieroglyphics, statues, and other artifacts, which have been found just the way they were left.

The oldest and largest of the pyramids is Cheops. It took its builders ten years just to level the land, and another twenty-three to raise the pyramid itself. There are more than two million blocks of limestone in Cheops alone, each weighing two and a half tons. Masons, stonecutters, and approximately a hundred-thousand slaves moved, lifted, and placed the stones 479 feet high. It's unimaginable how difficult it must have been to build the pyramids without modern tools, technology, or machines.

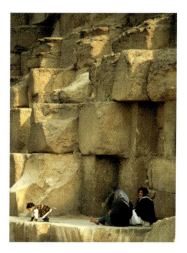

Cheops' giant limestone blocks

Back in the day, the planners must have over-ordered supplies because when Cheops was completed, there was an abundance of leftover stone. They used the twenty thousand tons of excess limestone to build the Sphinx. The feline-man symbolizes the union and power of strength and intelligence—a lion's body with a god's face, topped with the royal headdress of Egypt. The Sphinx is fifty meters long and twenty-two meters high, carved entirely from one piece of that leftover stone.

The Sphinx

Opening My Cultural Lens

Bookkeeper in Old Cairo

What happened to the Sphinx's nose? Some think it was destroyed in the fifteenth century by Muhammad Sa'im al-Dahr, a fanatic Muslim leader who found out peasants were worshipping the Sphinx. Peeved with their blatant display of idolatry, it is said that Sa'im al-Dahr whacked off the Sphinx's nose. He was later lynched for vandalism. Others believe that during the eighteenth century, some of Napoleon's soldiers fired a cannonball and hit the nose. Yet others reckon during the Ottoman Empire, the Turks used the face for target practice. It could also have been destroyed by erosion or a natural disaster, but that explanation isn't as much fun.

Mudbrick homes along the Nile

Tending the laundry

My curiosity about Egypt's history took me about four hundred miles south of Cairo to Luxor, the Valley of the Kings. This is where most of the major pharaohs lived, ruled, and were buried. Originally named Thebes, the four-thousand-year-old city includes historic tombs and temples such as the Karnak Temple, a main place of worship and one of the largest religious temples ever built; and the Luxor Temple, also known as the Harem of the South (what happens in Luxor, stays in Luxor).

Farther south, near the border of Sudan, are the temples of Abu Simbel. They fea-

Luxor Temple

Karnak Temple

ture two colossal statues of Ramses II. He had the temples built, then he dedicated them to himself. Abu Simbel is considered one of

Opening My Cultural Lens

Abu Simbel temples

the world's greatest monuments. It was carved out of the mountain between 1290 and 1224 BC. Each statue is twenty meters high and has smaller statues of Nefertari, his wife, at their feet.

Before I left Egypt, there was one more thing to do: a night trek to the top of Mount Sinai to witness the spiritual sunrise. We first drove through the peaceful hillsides in the lower Sinai Peninsula to get to St. Catherine's Monastery, named after a martyr who was tortured on a spiked wheel for her Christianity. The monastery was founded on the traditional site of Moses' burning bush.

At 2:00 a.m., I began my hike—a pilgrimage made by Christians, Jews, and Muslims—so I'd arrive at the summit to photograph the morning's new light. It was late November, just before Ramadan, and there was just a sliver of the moon for light. My Bedouin guide sometimes had to steer me by the arm because I couldn't see my hand in front of my face. Only the bright stars guided us, no thanks to a pitiful flashlight that needed a new battery. Fortunately, I had good knees back then because the trek up 3,750 steps, called the Steps of Penitence, took three long hours.

We reached the summit in the pre-dawn hours when the temperature remained cold. When the sky slowly lightened in soft shades of blue and yellow, I knew I was in for something special. As the sun peeked out to clip the mountain tops, the hills erupted in deep hues of orange, creating a sunrise even more breathtaking than expected.

Spiritual sunrise, Mount Sinai

    I didn't appreciate how tough the climb up was until I came back down in daylight and could actually see the terrain. My toes dug into my hiking boots as I carefully navigated the descent. As the sun rose, the once-nippy air abruptly turned dry and hot.

    I pondered the ties that Jesus, Moses, and Muhammad had to Mount Sinai, which is where Moses received the Ten Commandments from God and where a covenant between God and his people was established. I was starting to get all philosophical about the spiritual significance when I drifted off, thinking, *Geez, I'm starving and could use a bath.*

Formidable rainforest

AMAZON

*Yes, It Was Me.
I Disrupted the Ecosystem*

I struggled to get my long legs into the cramped cockpit of the tiny two-seater airplane. I quickly looked over my shoulder to make sure my bags were crammed in the back, and then we were off—to the Amazon.

By now, I had visited several places so isolated that people would ask, where in the heck is that? My plan was to spend a month in the Amazon learning about different indigenous groups that live in the dense, secluded jungle—groups whose fragile cultures were at risk. The trip began by chartering a small airplane that took me to a carved-out runway so deep in the rainforest that the closest dirt road was nearly 150 miles away—a four-day walk for a local.

When I wasn't mesmerized by every dial on the control panel my knees were bent against, I took in the exhilarating bird's-eye view of endless jungles and winding brown rivers. We seemed to have flown forever.

Opening My Cultural Lens

As we began our descent, I thought I'd finally see a village or some people, but no, there were only trees. Lower and lower we slid, still no runway in sight. *Where in the world is he gonna put this thing down*, I almost said out loud. I swear we were at tree-top level when I saw what I prayed was a runway. Our pilot banked, leveled off, and suddenly, just like that, we were on the ground, bouncing down a grassy patch that had been cleared with a machete, no doubt, for our little airplane. Where the people came from was beyond me, but there they were: men, women, and children, all fascinated with the little machine that just dropped from the sky carrying a goofy white lady with a camera.

Landing on the jungle's carved-out runway

Welcome Wagon

As quickly as we landed, I was ushered down a path to the river, tossed my bags into a small dug-out canoe, and said hello to my guide, Uwiti. I planned to spend the next ten days in a small village in the Kapawi Reserve of the Ecuadorian Amazon. It was home to the Achuar people. Only two thousand Achuar remained in Ecuador, and they were the last indigenous group in the country to have contact with the outside world. The first contact with the Achuar only happened in the '70s.

Transportation

It was steaming hot and ridiculously humid, yet I needed to cover my arms and legs to prevent the armies of tiny flies and sand fleas called *arenillas* from eating me alive. It was a small price to pay for being transported into another world bursting with little-known traditions and rituals.

I stayed in a little building in a room with the all-important mosquito net. At night it was pitch black. Trees shrouded the village, so the moon and stars provided little light. My room had a generator that ran on solar power, but the sun struggled to break through to charge it. There was no hot water. I had to make sure everything in my room was zipped up tight because of some pesky little roaches, large spiders, and God knows what else. All these darn bugs will get into everything. Likewise, my hiking boots and knee-high rubber boots hung upside down.

The first night was a learning experience. I tossed my flashlight and a bottle of water under the mosquito net because I didn't want to have to search for them during the night. Next to my bed was a nightstand, where I placed a couple of pills that managed the unwanted hot flashes which plagued me at that point of my life. In my dark and otherwise quiet room, I heard all kinds of new sounds and scratching noises—insects and animals—all scratching! I knew there was nothing I could do, and I wasn't too hip to what I might see, so I didn't point my flashlight around. The next morning, I reached toward the nightstand to take my pills only to find a residue where they had been placed. *Oh God,* I thought in horror, *something has eaten my hormones, and now I am single-handedly responsible for disrupting the ecosystem.*

The Amazon's complex ecosystem provides the Achuar with all they need. The forest is their soul, and all

Uwiti

life has meaning and importance. Plants provide countless medicinal and narcotic benefits and are used by the Achuar to heal everything from cuts and infections to muscle cramps.

Every morning began at sunrise. The Amazon's transportation system is an extensive network of tributaries, and other than hours-long hiking, it's the only way to get around. I put on my good old rubber boots and hopped into a canoe to visit a village or two situated on or near the river, each located miles and miles from the next.

My purpose for visiting was to meet and photograph indigenous families, and traveling with a local guide was the only way I could gain access. Even with his able assistance, getting to any given village was an arduous, often all-day effort. In addition to river journeys, the trips required long treks in the wet jungle, clearing our way with machetes through thick vines and branches, walking over makeshift bridges, and sloshing through muddy waters. I often got so stuck in the peanut butter-like mud that my guide would have to pull me out by yanking on my tall rubber boots. Have I mentioned the oppressive heat, the dripping humidity, and the relentless insects? Scratching, scratching, always scratching, I had to stay covered because of the stinging bugs. I felt like I was encased in a plastic bag that wouldn't breathe, sometimes so overheated I could faint. *This is what hell must be like*, I thought. *Just kill me now*.

Each ethnic group, and usually each tribe, speaks its own distinct language, making communications quite entertaining. In my conversations, the translation process began in English, moved to Spanish, then settled into the local language. If there was a second tribal language involved, translations got so twisted sometimes no one knew what the other was talking about.

At long last, we arrived at my first Achuar village. I had anticipated this moment for so long, my curiosity and anxiety were rising. This isolated place in the middle of the jungle—its mysterious people and their strange customs—the environment rattled my nerves, making my stomach a bit queasy. I suddenly got awfully thirsty, and my palms were sweating as we approached the outskirts of the village. Here we go.

Gaining permission to enter the village, never mind being allowed to photograph anyone, was quite a process. I was required to make a traditional, formal presentation to the village elder or chief, who had agreed to see me because he thought I might let others in the outside world know how the aggressive expansion of oil exploration in the area is infringing on their sacred homeland. Uwiti and I, along with another fellow who spoke this particular tribe's native language,

Opening My Cultural Lens

Village chief's home

Tashim

entered through the back of the chief's home, a twenty by sixty-foot hut—just a roof on posts without walls.

We sat quietly in the back on a bench. The chief, named Tashim, sat on an ordinary yet officious chair in the middle of the room nearly twenty feet away, whittling a piece of wood. For more than ten minutes, he did not acknowledge us or speak to us. It was a long time to just sit there saying nothing. I kept looking over at the translator, who just nodded as if to say, *just be patient*.

Tashim's wife was in the kitchen in the women's part of the house, making chicha, a fermented manioc-based drink that is a huge part of the culture. She mashed it, chewed it, and spit what she had chewed back into the mixture. When chicha is served, it is customary to take the bowl and hold it in your hands, though you don't have to drink it. It's con-

Bowl of fermented chicha

sidered extremely offensive *not* to accept the bowl. After the chewing and spitting part, aside from the fact that it was made with unpurified water, I chose only to take a sip. It tasted like dirty socks. We sat in silence with our bowls of chicha, waiting for the elder to speak.

Finally, Tashim casually began chatting with our translator in their common language. Uwiti and I just sat there. Another five minutes went by. Then, suddenly, the translator jumped up and said, "He's ready!" meaning, let the presentation begin.

Tashim would start. He wanted to know where I lived (and where in the world Minnesota was), how many children I had, my age, and what had brought me to his house. In short, who I was, and why was I here. Because of the multiple translations, some context was lost along the arduous way, so right off the bat, I knew our conversation would be choppy at best.

Then it was my turn to make my presentation. I could remain seated. I tried to answer his questions, but Tashim, who has eight children, could not comprehend that I was single with no kids. That concept was completely foreign to his native culture. I was pretty used to this reaction. It's typical for me to encounter various traditions around the world where girls, through pre-arranged marriages, produce lots and lots of children. I attempted to explain that being single with no kids gave me the freedom to travel. He didn't seem to accept that, though he never said anything. He asked me where I get money. I explained I was self-employed—a woman providing for herself was another concept not understood in his culture. He continued to stare at me.

After well over an hour into the presentation, the translator said the chief accepted my answers to his questions. Now, it was my turn to ask him questions, which, again, were all translated twice. Tashim's answers described customs involving his home and family, and indeed their struggle with the oil companies that want to drill in their area. The translator said the chief would appreciate the world knowing about his people, the precious rainforest, and the oil problems.

Thankfully, Tashim accepted my full presentation and not only allowed me to stay for more chicha, but to take a couple of photos as well. I think he liked me because he wanted to play me a song on his flute. I was deeply honored to be a guest in his home. To experience firsthand his fascinating, ancient culture was simply unforgettable.

Uwiti told me a story of how the Achuar get their strength through the rainforest, and how some follow a ceremony to attain it. They first clear a spot next to a waterfall and fast for three days. Then, they'll drink guayusa, an herbal beverage made from mixing a native caffeinated holly with tobacco. The tobacco makes them throw up, purifying their body and eliminating all things that are bad. Oftentimes, the Achuar will continue this ceremony by drinking a powerful hallucinogenic called *ayahuasca*. This further purifies the body but also helps them obtain a vision of what they'll face next in their life.

The Achuar have a long history of inter-tribal battles. When warriors would prepare to fight, they'd begin by painting their faces with symbols that represent worshipped animals, crocodiles, snakes, and items in the forest that they believe give them strength.

Hanging Lobster Claw plant

Marriages are pre-arranged in many of these cultures. Uwiti explained that after a young man selects his bride, he meets with his father, who meets with the girl's father to discuss the situation. Then, the fathers drink the guayusa, throw up, get purified, and hopefully bless the marriage. I also learned that *all* physical relations take place outside the house, usually in the rainforest.

At another village, I met with the elder, who is also a shaman. After the now-familiar formal presentation, I asked how a person becomes a shaman. The man explained that at age twenty, he began meeting with an elder shaman for guidance, and the two drank the guayusa, threw up, and got purified. Then the elder shaman put his saliva in the drink to give the new shaman strength, followed by both men drinking the potent hallucinogenic ayahuasca. They would experience visions about the village and community, its problems, and how to cure them.

When treating a person medically, a shaman first meets with the patient to determine the illness or injury. If the ailment is not immediately understood or visible, the shaman will drink the ayahuasca to envision the problem and determine its cure.

Fewer and fewer men become shamans anymore. The main reason is that their lives are always at risk. As the key leaders in the middle of local conflicts, shamans are believed to both cure and kill through magical means. The shamans manipulate the good and bad spirits and, therefore, can be accused of steering those spirits. Some folks just don't like the outcomes, so the shamans are always looking over their shoulders.

The next morning, I said adios to my hosts and flew in a little two-seater Cessna to a small airport near Puyo, which is in central Ecuador, to meet up with my next guide, Yaanua. She would be with me during my entire stay in Miazal, where I would become acquainted with the Shuar indigenous people. Yaanua grew up in this area, located in the Morona-Santiago province on the Peruvian border. This area is even more remote than Kapawi, and I could not find Miazal on any map.

After landing on a grassy runway and hiking to a canoe, we were off again down a river to the village. There was no lodge. Instead, I stayed with a family. The head of the household was Ernesto; he would be my native guide. He and his wife, Juanita, had seven kids. Yaanua spoke English, Spanish, and the native language, though no one else in the village spoke English.

In this village, there was no electricity, solar power, or hot water. My guest room had no screens on the windows, so my mosquito net was my only refuge. It became my little cave.

Opening My Cultural Lens

Traditional Shuar village

This family loved to laugh! They'd hoot and holler, tease each other and tell jokes—and it was contagious. I had no idea what they were saying or laughing about most of the time (likely it was at my expense), but I found myself laughing right along.

It doesn't get any hotter than being on the equator, or any wetter than being in the rainforest. The air doesn't move. I was tormented by microscopic bugs with bites that burned like fire ants. I easily had more than a hundred bites, but who's counting? All I know is I wanted to scream. I had never felt so miserable in my life, yet onward we slogged.

My host family, always laughing

The village had a school and a little church, which combined Christianity and the Shuar's traditional spiritual practice. The kids only spoke Shuar but were learning Spanish.

Ernesto's five-year-old son, Davíd, became my pal. I adored him, and he followed me everywhere. Hand-in-hand, we were together all the time. I'd often sit with him after school so he could practice his Spanish, a language I butchered. I'm certain my pathetic junior high instruction set back his progress, but we were inseparable. Each morning at sunrise, I'd tiptoe over to his house and say, "*Davíd, vamos al rio?*" He'd come flying out the door, and we'd set out to take a swim. The water was a glorious relief.

My everpresent companion, Davíd

One day we hiked three hours to a different village to visit another Shuar family. When we finally arrived at the edge of the village, Ernesto announced us by shouting out some kind of signal. (I think it was probably a warning, as in, *here she comes!*)

The chief's name was Tarira, and his wife was Mamatui. They had eleven kids. We entered the back of their home and I gave my same presentation to the chief, who was seated twenty feet away. The process was less formal than in Kapawi, probably because Yaanua, Ernesto, the chief, and his wife seemed to know one another. They began talking right away, and in no time, they were laughing uproariously! Mamatui began serving chicha, which she had prepared in a large kettle for our arrival. Here, it's custom that no one leaves until the chicha is gone. More than three hours later, they (not me) were all getting toasted on the fermented drink, laughing up a storm. At some point, we were served lunch, which included chicken, hearts of palm, and plantain, cooked and served in a large leaf. We ate with our fingers off the ground next to our muddy boots.

Tarira

Tarira thought it would be a grand idea to teach me how to use a blowgun—this after a boatload of Amazonian moonshine. Under the tutelage of one of the villager experts, I was instructed to place the dart in the end of the weapon, the side that you put in your mouth. Next, I put some cotton next to the dart to seal it and to create pressure.

Teeth from the killer piranha are used to indent the end of the dart, Yaanua explained.

Facepaint initiation

If the targeted animal breaks it off, the poisoned part of the tip remains intact. I'm not sure that was helpful, using deadly poison and all, but I was then told to just aim and blow. At one point, I was sure I shot his chicken. After a little practice, I did well enough to win the chief's praise. My victory lap concluded with Ernesto painting my face with red dye to make me look a bit more imposing. It wasn't my best look, but I was officially pronounced a warrior.

By then, it was late in the afternoon, and I learned Ernesto had prearranged with his "neighbor" (though I had no idea, in this area, how far away a neighbor lives) to paddle his canoe upstream to pick us up and bring us back. *Thank God*, I almost said out loud, as I didn't think I could bear another three-hour hike home. But first, the neighbor joined our festivities for a few bowls of chicha. These characters obviously take happy hour seriously. It was getting darker now, and I was wondering how these two drunken sailors were going to get us back home safely. Their technique was to stand as they paddled, which might have been fine under normal circumstances, but in this case, the canoe rocked precipitously, mostly because the boys were a bit loopy, the sky was getting darker, and they were laughing so hard.

After ten days here, I felt a part of this crazy, happy family. But it was time to say goodbye to my new friends and to my little pal, Davíd. Yaanua, the pilot, and I had one additional passenger on the way back: a duck. I think it was going to be someone's Christmas dinner.

Students taking a break, Miazal

The last leg of my Amazon trip was to a small lodge on the Napo River, a main tributary of the Amazon, to learn about the Quechua indigenous group. One of my most interesting village visits was with a healer named Bajuyuk. He was a medicine man, but not a shaman. Bajuyuk and his wife had twelve kids. Three, he told me, had died.

Ernesto

To mark my visit, they held a traditional cleansing ceremony. The healer wore a headdress made from vines and bird feathers. These crowns are sacred and not to be reproduced by anyone for any other purpose. The healer's powers are passed down through his ancestors. Bajuyuk's wife burned beeswax in a pot to create smoke. The ceremony aims to collect the bad energy, concentrate it in the *malaria panga* leaf, and blow away the negative energy.

Bajuyuk, the healer

Juan, my guide, participated in the ceremony first, then it was my turn. Following Juan's guidance, I sat on a chair in the middle of the room and closed my eyes to concentrate. Then the healer smoked some tobacco and gently blew the smoke at me, including at my face and around my head. Then he waved the malaria panga all over me, head to toe, to collect bad energy and concentrate it in the leaves, softly chanting all the while. Then, the healer blew the bad spirits away. I hope he got them all.

Juan was a relatively serious man, probably in his mid-thirties. He told me a number of fantastical stories about shamanism.

Cleansing ceremony with Juan

Three years prior, his father, who lives in a remote village, had a stroke. Juan's family had converted to Christianity and no longer acknowledged shamanism. Juan needed to arrange to have his father airlifted to a hospital. He spent everything he had to transport his father to the hospital, where he stayed for seventeen days before the doctors gave up and sent him home to die. Juan, who was not a Christian, begged his mother to take his father to a shaman. With nothing to lose, she reluctantly agreed. The shaman said he'd see him in exchange for a hammock, a hunting dog, and a blowgun.

After the first consultation to determine the illness, the shaman lit some tobacco and waved the smoke all over Juan's father. Then he drank the ayahuasca to have a vision to locate the problem. Next, the shaman told Juan he was going to concentrate on his father's body in two areas, his throat and in his rib cage. The shaman bit into his father's throat, Juan said, and sucked out . . . a three-inch centipede! Then, the shaman bit into his rib cage and sucked out a small twig that had hair wrapped around it. The western doctors had sent him home to die, but three years later, Juan's father remained alive and well.

How did the centipede and twig get into his father's body? Who knows. It's impossible to understand, and whether I believe it or not is not important. The point is that Juan and his father did. They believed this was an evil spirit sent by another shaman on behalf of someone who had ill feelings toward Juan's father and wanted to make something bad happen. It is a prime example of why fewer men are willing to take on the risk that comes with being a shaman.

My head was spinning, and I could only stare at Juan as he told me this story. He understood my skepticism, yet he knew I respected his feelings. And he wasn't finished. One night when Juan was a baby, he suddenly started screaming uncontrollably and developed a bad fever. His parents took him to the shaman. After the ayahuasca, the shaman sucked a bunch of beetles from Juan's chest. He showed me his scars. By this time, I felt like I'd taken the ayahuasca!

My Amazon adventure had come to an end. Admittedly, this trip was a little more challenging than I expected, but I got a rare glimpse into the lives of three extraordinary groups of indigenous people, and among the wonders that stood out was the importance of family. Every home was made up of extended family members—sons and their wives, daughters and their husbands—along with many children. People hold their elders in the highest regard because they're the link to their ancestors.

Amazon basin's hundreds of tributaries

For me, being submerged in the Amazon punctuated how critical our earth's ecosystem is, and how one environment affects the entire planet. I learned how the indigenous have a harmonic relationship with the rainforest and its creatures, acting as custodians of the environment. Sacred animals are never hunted or eaten. These groups are among countless indigenous people whose cultures could be eliminated by development encroaching on the rainforest. Oil, commercial ranching, agriculture, mining, and deforestation all make the rainforest and its people vulnerable.

Few places on Earth have a more staggering impact on the planet than the Amazon. While growing my geographic resume, I continued to sharpen my awareness of the interconnectedness of life. I guess I don't need to be a Buddhist philosopher to grasp this worldview, but the more I travel, the more I witness this concept in practice.

GUATEMALA

I Speak Fluent Pantomime

Over the years, I visited a number of breathtaking Latin American destinations, some multiple times. There is so much to see and do, from the islands of the Caribbean, to Mexico and Central America in the north, through the steamy jungles of the Amazon, and down the spine of the Andes mountains to Patagonia's pointed peaks and granite spires, glaciers, and icefields. They are all magnificent.

Centuries of colonization and slave-trading resulted in a seemingly infinite mix of ethnic groups and races, each preserving its captivating traditions and practices. One of Latin America's most colorful countries is Guatemala, the heart of the ancient Mayan Empire and home to one of the strongest indigenous cultures in the Americas.

Sadly, like many parts of Latin America, Guatemala's history includes decades of civil war that only ended in 1996. As recently as the early '80s, the dictator Efraín Ríos Montt exterminated the inhabitants of four hundred villages. More than two hundred thousand men of Mayan descent were tortured and slaughtered, and one hundred thousand women were raped. In 2012, Rios Montt was convicted of crimes against humanity. The country has tried to recover from the genocide but continues to suffer from political instability, unemployment, corruption, and scandals.

Against this backdrop of unrest, Guatemala is culturally rich. With more than two dozen ethnic Mayan groups, twenty-three different languages, numerous heritage sites, Spanish colonial towns, rainforests, and thirty-three volcanoes, Guatemala is a photographer's delight. And did I mention the vivid, multicolored clothing? I began by heading north to a major epicenter of the Mayan civilization, Tikal.

Traditional Mayan dress, Santiago

Guatemala

For hundreds of years, a lush jungle covered this huge complex of ruins. In 1848, a team of archaeologists began working to uncover what has become the largest excavated site in Latin America. Tikal once supported one hundred thousand Mayans and boasted more than three thousand separate buildings and two hundred monuments and altars dating from 600 BC to 900 AD.

Tikal

Farther south in Nebaj, my guide and I happened upon hundreds of women carrying signs—a demonstration protesting violence against women. This was a small town, and the protests were going on right in front of a Catholic Church. This was a very gutsy act in this male-dominated society. Many of the women were either victims themselves, or were mourning the loss of family or friends, or both. I was proud to join hundreds of my courageous sisters that day.

Protesting violence against women, Nebaj

Headdress worn by a local weaver, Santa Catarina

In the highlands, we went to Chichicastenango to learn more about the area's fascinating spiritual practice called syncretism, which combines Catholicism with Mayan indigenous shamanistic practices. Worshipping with both a Catholic priest and a Mayan shaman, indigenous people at prayer burn candles, swing incense, and chant to honor their ancestors. On the fringe of town is the Chi-Chi cemetery, filled with brightly painted mausoleums and above-ground crypts. The crypts are either owned, in which case they're yours forever, or they can be rented, in which case, eventually, your bones will be relocated.

Mayans practice syncretism in parts of Guatemala.

Colorful cemetery, Chichicastenango

During this trip, I stayed for a couple of days with a family in Totonicapán. Miguel and Rachael share their modest home with their three kids and eighty-eight-year-old grandmother. Miguel is a fifth-generation weaver, and Rachael is a nurse at a women's clinic. She leaves the house each morning at six o'clock, walks two hours into the mountains, works eight hours, then walks two hours home—only to cook and take care of the kids. Without complaint, she does it all over again the next day.

We may have shared the limited space in their house, but we did not share a common language. They spoke no English and my Spanish *está patética!* Our conversations were hysterical. At dinner one night, Miguel asked about my family. Right off the bat, I attempted to explain that no, I am not married and never have been. No kids.

"*Ah,*" he said politely. I think he understood. *That went pretty well.*

Then Miguel asked if I have siblings. Yes, I have a sister (Jean, *Juana*) and a brother (Bill, *Guillermo*). So far, my Spanish was working. Miguel wanted to hear more. I told him my sister is involved in the theater and acts in local productions. Exceedingly impressed, Miguel turned to Rachael, clapped his hands alongside his cheeks and exclaimed, *"El teatro! Ah, el teatro!"* They both thought my sister was the famous Juana Shore, a Broadway and Hollywood star, and were wondering why a celebrity wasn't sitting at their table instead of me. *No sé.*

Next, they asked about my brother. I explained, or so I thought, that Bill has had a long, successful career working for a big liquor distributor. Sadly, my limited Spanish again did not serve me (or my brother) well because they looked at me with sympathetic, yet squinted eyes. I think they heard me say, "*Mi hermano is a very large man who drinks too much.*" I knew I would later have some explaining to do with Guillermo. *Lo siento.*

Musicians everywhere

CUBA

— *Che, Castro, and Hemingway's Bartender* —

I could have entered Cuba illegally through Canada or Mexico, but I didn't want to do that, especially since I was now managing a nonprofit and didn't feel comfortable skirting the system. In 2009, President Barack Obama lifted the fifty-year-old US travel embargo and granted State Department-sanctioned licenses to a few US companies to conduct cultural programs in Cuba. Finally, this was my chance, though I'd have to travel with a group, on a bus. I always travel alone, so the thought of being joined at the hip with a busload of others was not my cup of tea. I had no choice.

Everyone has their own impressions of Cuba. I thought it would appear impoverished and oppressed, replete with reminders of Castro's dominance. It didn't. That's not to say people aren't economically challenged. They most definitely are. When I was there, the average professional's salary was about twenty dollars a month. Many educated Cubans, such as doctors, leave to take jobs in Europe or

Opening My Cultural Lens

other countries in Latin America. If they choose to stay and work, they might drive a taxi or take another second job to get by.

The best place to begin to understand Cuba today is with the oligarch Fulgencio Batista, who presided over a brutal regime in the early '50s. Overrun by gangsters and corruption, Cuba was ripe for a revolution. The first attempt to overthrow Batista came in 1953. A young rebel leader, Fidel Castro, began to speak about la revolución. To plan it, he fled to Mexico, where he met up with his brother, Raul, and with Ernesto "Che" Guevara. Fidel may have been the brains behind the revolution, but Che gave it sex appeal. Of course, he also eventually became the perfect martyr for this country. He was courageous, rugged, and handsome. Che and the Castro brothers recruited peasants who were promised land reforms in exchange for their support. By 1959 the guerrilla army was nine thousand strong. Led by Che, the rebels overthrew Batista.

The sign says, "Your Example Lives. Your Ideas Endure."

Hated by some, worshipped by others, Castro nationalized Cuban society. He reduced rents, reformed farming, began to eliminate illiteracy, and provided universal healthcare and education. But the government took over utilities, and private land and businesses, many of which were owned by Americans, without compensation. The media were under state control, and those opposed to the new government were sent to labor camps. In 1961, the United States enacted a trade embargo against Cuba and decided it was time to overthrow Castro. The Bay of Pigs Invasion lasted seventy-two hours before the Cubans turned back the US-backed forces.

The following year brought the Cuban Missile Crisis. Because of the American embargo, Cuba's biggest trading partner was the Soviet Union, which (pun intended) had its arms around Cuba. On the island and on ships offshore, Castro allowed the USSR to deploy dozens of nuclear missiles pointed at US cities, creating a standoff that brought us to the edge of a nuclear war. Kennedy demanded the missiles be dismantled, and the world waited for six days until Soviet strongman Nikita Khrushchev finally turned his warships around.

The possibility of a nuclear war was real and scared most people to death. I remember the "duck and cover" exercises in school, where we scrambled under our desks to protect ourselves from a nuclear attack. We were terrified, and teachers and parents had no reassuring explanations to offer. I remember one of my teachers saying, "Your assignment, if we are here tomorrow . . ." When I told my parents what she said, all they could do was shake their heads. They, too, didn't know what to say.

Pensive shopkeeper, central Cuba

The collapse of the Soviet Union in 1990 was devastating to Cuba, which suddenly had no fuel, power, or transportation, and little food. Castro wanted to ease some of the economic pressures, so he allowed Cubans to leave the country. And they did. More than thirty-thousand people, including children, set out on homemade rafts in shark-filled waters, headed to South Florida. Ever since, different US administrations have gone back and forth on whether to normalize relations with Cuba.

When Fidel Castro's health began to fail, Raul became president. The younger Castro lifted restrictions on Cubans owning TVs, computers, and cell phones, and allowed individuals to own their own businesses.

Obama finally reinstated the "people-to-people" license to visit Cuba, a travel category that promoted educational dialogue between American and Cuban people. When I was there, it looked like US sanctions against Cuba might be eased soon, but what progress was made by the Obama Administration was quickly erased by the election of Donald Trump. Hope, today, is that President Joe Biden will normalize US relations and lift diplomatic and economic sanctions.

Restored classics

Because of the lengthy embargo, there are no newer American cars, but who needs them when the enterprising Cubans maintain the classic cars of the '40s and '50s? Everywhere I went, I enjoyed seeing beautifully restored cars from my childhood, including my favorite 57 Chevy. In those glory days, cars came in pastel shades of salmon, aqua, and lime, as well as vibrant pink, orange, and yellow. The American classics have been carefully cared for by gifted Cuban mechanics who somehow fix the imports with improvised parts made from scrap metal. It's like a car museum!

Many of the same brilliant hues proudly decorate Cuba's colonial buildings, some dating back to the sixteenth century, when the Spanish conquered the island. Art Deco and Art Nouveau archi-

Busy outdoor square, Havana

tectural styles were introduced in the 1930s and continued to be built until the 1959 revolution. Stained glass, shuttered doors, courtyards, and wooden and wrought-iron window grilles and balconies all reflect Cuba's decadent, pre-revolution years. The buildings need a lot of TLC, but I saw a fair amount of restoration in an attempt to preserve history as well as to replace the simply awful post-revolution Soviet construction.

In addition to their outstanding architecture, Cubans are famous for their world-renowned art. In fact, each province in Cuba has a school that grooms kids in all areas of the arts: paint, design, poetry, writing, guitar-playing, and even more remote skills, like bongo, are taught there.

Street dancers

And of course, there is the music—extraordinary music—salsa, rumba, mambo, and other energetic mixes of Cubans' African, Spanish, and French heritage. Just like the rest of Latin America, from Rio de Janeiro to Buenos Aires to Santiago, music here is omnipresent, infectious, and more fun than should be legal. Wherever you go—streets, restaurants, homes, courtyards—people enjoy live music. At a restaurant, I'd watch in amazement as an ordinary couple just decided to get up in the middle of their dinner and do the tango. Then, I'd turn around and hear a trio playing a Tito Puente tune as they entertained on a street corner, sparking more spontaneous dancing. And over there, sitting in a stairwell, I'd see a solo guitarist already drawing a crowd. Music might explain why Cubans have such happy personalities.

Happy dispositions

We—when I say we, I mean our busload—visited more World Heritage sites, including Cienfuegos, a port city and historic center, and Trinidad, one of Cuba's finest colonial towns. We also stopped at several rural schools, where we learned more about how Cuba has done an impressive job of nearly eliminating illiteracy. According to the Ministry of Education, Cuba has made a serious investment in public education, which is free from the cradle to the grave, including universities and trade schools.

Palacio de Valle, Cienfuegos   Artist, Havana   Playful student, Santiago

Cuba's largest religion is Catholic, though others are practiced. One of the most intriguing is Santería, an Afro-Caribbean religion that combines Catholicism and African beliefs observed by slaves. The religion focuses on building relationships between people and spirits, called orisha, who are a manifestation of God.

We rounded out the trip in Havana. One nice perk of traveling with this tour group was the first-class accommodations. I was not used to that. We all

Santería

checked into the Hotel Nacional de Cuba, a spectacular art deco structure that exhibits all the elegance that attracted personalities and celebrities back in the '30s, '40s, and '50s. From Frank Sinatra to

Winston Churchill, it was *the* place people wanted to be seen in Havana. I walked through the grand entrance and into the elaborate lobby, where I noticed a placard that read, "Saturday: Buena Vista Social Club." I am nuts about Cuban music and adore this group. Lucky for me, it was Saturday! I was so excited, I almost got hiccups.

Spontaneous dancing

For the uninitiated, the Buena Vista Social Club is an ensemble that was popular in the '40s and '50s during the peak of Havana's nightclub scene. The group, which today has been reintroduced to a world stage, was forced to shut down in 1959 when Castro closed Cuba's clubs. And on that Saturday night in one of the hotel's ornate ballrooms, the show featured fourteen musicians—including a few from the original ensemble—plus some spicy red-hot salsa dancers. The music was so infectious, the show was more like a big party. Everyone in the audience, including me, was on their feet dancing.

In addition to visiting a couple hospitals in Havana, our group stopped by a national cemetery. One of the most interesting sites there was the tomb of Hemingway's bartender. Hemingway lived in Havana for twenty years when he wrote *For Whom the Bell Tolls* and *The Old Man and the Sea*. Hemingway had a reputation for being fond of the drink. His bartender must have been quite the guy.

I loved Cuba. I loved the architecture, the cars, and of course, the people and their music. If I wasn't singing "Chan Chan" before Havana, I certainly couldn't get the tune out of my head after Saturday night. I also enjoyed my new travel buddies and the posh accommodations, but I needed to get off the bus.

INDIA

Two-Sided Mirror

It took me some time before I felt I had gained a mature enough perspective to go to India. Even without having been there, I knew I needed to form a stronger crust, so to speak, so I could face its poverty, disease, pollution, and poor hygiene. The numbers are staggering. The population is pushing 1.4 billion. Nearly two-thirds of Indian households in 2020 lived on less than $2 a day. Millions are homeless, and women and children suffer the most. While I knew it wouldn't be easy, I needed to visit the world's oldest democracy.

Wanting to go on yet another safari, I also planned excursions to two tiger camps. But I began my trip in Delhi, which is divided into Old Delhi, the historic part of the city, and New Delhi, the capital. In 2020, its combined population was a whopping 30.3 million people. Heavy industry, waste- and crop-burning, chronic dust, and emissions from millions of cars and two-wheelers have helped Delhi become the most polluted urban conglomeration in the world,

Opening My Cultural Lens

according to the World Health Organization. These are not the kind of highlights any chamber of commerce boasts about. Yet, alongside this dreadful backdrop, chaotic New Delhi has another face—one that is rich with wonderful thousand-year-old palaces and monuments of Indo-Muslim architecture.

Delhi's choked streets

India is 80 percent Hindu and nearly 15 percent Muslim. I visited the Jama Masjid Mosque, India's largest. This center of the Muslim community can accommodate twenty thousand worshippers. The nearby Red Fort is a palace that became the hub of the Mughal Empire in the seventeenth century. Delhi's most famous landmark is the Qutb Minar, or "victory tower," built in 1193 to celebrate Islam's victory over the city's last Hindu ruler.

Jama Masjid

One of my most lasting impressions of New Delhi was visiting the Gandhi Memorial, where I learned more about Mahatma Gandhi, who tried to get the Hindus and Muslims to lay aside their differences and unify. But first, he understood that India's Islamic community needed to have its own homeland. The 1947 Partition of India divided the two religious groups into two nations: Muslim Pakistan and Hindu India. Instead of a solution, the arrangement turned into a nightmare.

Hindus and Muslims alike found themselves in partitioned states where neither could afford nor agree

India

Praying at mosque, Old Delhi

to be a minority. Millions of Hindus and Sikhs in the newly created Pakistan headed to India, and millions of Muslims in India moved to Pakistan. The two groups already had a long history of violence, and when the hostility between them exploded, it touched off one of the largest exoduses in human history, which in turn ignited a genocide of inexplicable savagery. Two million died, and a hundred thousand women were abducted, tortured, and raped.

The following year, Gandhi was assassinated by a Hindu fanatic who opposed the split. The intent of the 1947 partition was to advance peace by establishing two independent nations, but suspicion and conflict still exist today in the region of Kashmir, which sits on this northern border and is claimed by both countries.

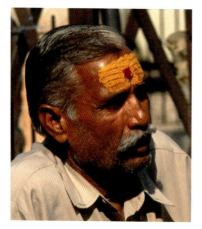

The tilak is a Hindu spiritual marking on forehead.

After a few days in New Delhi, I flew southeast to Khajuraho, a World Heritage site built by the Chandela Dynasty one thousand years ago. The three groups of temples are dedicated to the three principal Hindu gods: Brahma, The Creator; Vishnu, The Preserver; and Shiva, The Destroyer. The exquisitely carved temples are famous for another reason; they feature intricate erotic sculptures. There are lots of stories explaining this art, but one is that the King, who wanted to grow the kingdom, needed to convince consenting adults that sex was not shameful, so he thought he'd try erotic art to get everyone to multiply. And that they did.

Khajuraho's suggestive architecture

To reach Bandhavgarh National Park for my first tiger safari, my guide, Mahinder, and I drove eight hours to go a mere 140 miles on the worst roads I've ever seen. Most were so ruined by monsoon flooding that driving on the side of the road was often better than driving on the road itself. I will never again complain about Midwestern potholes. The ride was like driving over ski moguls, and our car's shocks were so worn out, it was a wonder the car didn't break down. In no time, my eyes were running, and my skin was covered with black diesel exhaust and dust. I expected India to be challenging. It did not disappoint.

Nothing could have prepared me for the noise. The constant horn blowing was deafening, and traffic was unimaginably disorganized, with cars and motorbikes coming from every possible direction. We were passing on the shoulders and plowing like a fullback up the middle of oncoming traffic, animals, and people. I was flying around in the back seat because there were no seatbelts. I could only hold on to the door handle, praying like my life depended on it. There's a saying in India: three of the most important things you need are a good horn, good brakes, and good luck!

Navigating chaotic streets

By the time I got to Bandhavgarh, I was filthy. I had a pounding migraine and hadn't eaten since a skinny piece of toast at breakfast. I could not turn my head and neck, as the whiplash from the drive

Opening My Cultural Lens

was too painful. I was just about in tears, all the time wondering, *Why do I do this?*

I had, I realized, two choices: I could whine about this riotous environment—about the assaults on my privileged, comfortable and orderly life—or I could suck it up. Open my eyes, ears, and mind, and accomplish what I came here for: to learn about this extraordinary culture and its people and traditions. I needed to embrace this experience to see what was on the other side. Relying on my Finnish heritage, now was the time to apply some *sisu*, a Finnish concept meaning grit, perseverance, and determination.

What I ultimately found was an exhilarating destination, exploding with sounds, smells, and colors that conquered my senses—more than I would have otherwise taken in had I fought the sensory onslaught. India's kaleidoscope of colors, the mystical symbolism of its religious rituals, and its vivid art, fabric, and architecture are a burst of celebration. The aroma of traditional foods and spices; the smoke of burning incense and camphor; and the sweet, pungent fragrance of flowers, all add to the sensory overload.

Upper-caste family

It also stank. Cow dung, urine, decay, and rotting garbage were unavoidable.

Welcome to India, a hectic and electrifying country jam-packed with folks living life to the fullest.

The air was clear and clean in Bandhavgarh, where our safari began before sunrise. The game park was created to further the development of "Project Tiger," launched by the Indian government and the World Wildlife Fund to keep the endangered cats from extinction. Tigers can live to be seventy years old; a female will have two to three litters in her lifetime. Tigers have a large kill about every six days, then they just lie around. Lazy and elusive, they're rare to see.

It wasn't until late in the afternoon on my third and last day in Bandhavgarh that we finally spotted a giant five-hundred-pound male tiger, sleeping on a hillside about seventy yards away. The sun had just set, and it was already too disappointingly dark to photograph him. As we drove back to camp, a different tiger suddenly appeared out of nowhere and ambled toward a group of jeeps packed with visitors that had just learned of the sighting. Even in the late-day darkness, the tiger's brilliant orange color trimmed in sharp black and white was spectacular. But because of his position in front of the jeeps, I couldn't get a photo.

My second tiger safari took me to Ranthambore National Park, where on the very first game run, we spotted a female tiger in the tall grass. It was just before sunrise and still very dark. Sadly, this tiger was the last I was to see. Although I have no decent photos to show for my days on safari, I was able to see three—though only three—of these majestic animals.

I flew on to Rajasthan, a state in northern India. I got into the town of Agra late in the afternoon and rushed to the Taj Mahal to shoot it before sunset. I enjoyed the late-afternoon glow, but also wanted to photograph the Taj at sunrise, under a softer, pink light. So, the next morning I dragged

Taj Mahal

my weary butt out of bed and hopped on a rickshaw—perhaps it was not the smartest choice given my aching neck and back, but it sounded like a good, "when-in-India" idea at the time.

During the sixteenth and seventeenth centuries, the most affluent and decadent era in India's history, Muslims were in power. It was the fifth Mughal, Shah Jahan, who built the Taj Mahal, the Seventh Wonder of the World. It took twenty-thousand artisans twenty-two years to build, and more than a thousand elephants were needed to transport tons of white marble and to work the construction pulleys. The Taj is perfectly symmetrical. Its huge domed mausoleum is flanked by four minarets, which lean outward four degrees so they won't ever fall inward. The structure was built as a final resting place for Shah Jahan's wife, Mumtaz, who died at age thirty-nine while giving birth to their fourteenth child.

We drove five hours west to Jaipur, the capital of Rajasthan. It's called the "pink city" because, in 1876, some of its buildings were painted pink to welcome the Prince of Wales. The city is known for its palaces, including Hawa Mahal, called "Palace of the Winds," because it was designed with 953 small windows to keep a breeze circulating inside. Afterward, I rode an elephant (another poor choice of transportation) to get to the Jal Mahal, the summer residence of the maharajas in the eighteenth century.

Hawa Mahal Palace

Wherever I go, I love to visit schools. I make a point of leaving a donation as an expression of gratitude, always after consulting with my guide to discuss if I should give money or school supplies. During one of my long drives, I visited an Indian grade school, met with the teachers, and spoke to the class. Afterward, the teachers and little kids all lined up and sang songs for me. Too cute.

At a rural middle school, however, I had a supremely awkward encounter. It was located close to Kashmir in the northern part of India near Pakistan, where, since the 1947 Partition, there's not been a lot of love lost between the Hindu majority and Muslim minority. No one spoke English except for a couple of the teachers. One asked me to talk to his class about American schools. The kids were very curious and attentive. Everyone I had met in India up to this point was friendly and respectful, but my translator at this school, an administrator, was looking for trouble. He peppered me with inappropriate questions—in front of the students. He was way out of line.

Hindu school prayer, northern India

"So, how much money do you make?" he asked. This rural school was located in an extremely poor area, and Americans, of course, are all thought to be millionaires. There was no good way to answer him, so I pretended I didn't understand the question. He then asked, "How do you teach morals in American schools?"

I replied, "We don't teach morals in school; we teach them at home."

Then he said, "Why does your president support Pakistan?" I smelled trouble.

Opening My Cultural Lens

"Well, look at the time," I replied, "we must be on our way." The principal, who clearly did not understand what was going on, invited me into his office to sign a guest book, and then gave me a flower and thanked me for coming. I could not get back in the car fast enough.

Finally, I headed north by train to the base of the Himalayas to visit Rishikesh and Haridwar—two of five holy cities in India where worshippers participate in ceremonies on the Ganges River. Because the Ganges is sacred, people collect its sacred water and place it on their prayer tables at home when they worship. Aarti, held each evening at sunset, honors the gods with the gift of bright light. Hindus light candles and torches, some splash into the river, and others pour the water on themselves, washing away their sins and sickness.

The holy ceremony of Aarti on the Ganges

Rishikesh is also the place where the Beatles studied transcendental meditation with Maharishi Mahesh Yogi. The town is still filled with spiritual seekers and a few leftover hippies, all practicing yoga based on ancient Indian wisdom. I did seek some help from a local yogi, who gave me a little relaxation exercise to ease the worsening pain in my neck.

Next door to Rishikesh is Haridwar, which means God's Door, a place where Hindus believe they can pass directly into the celestial realm. We drove up a mountain to a temple. Along the way, I bought offerings of incense and flowers. I was invited into the temple by the priest, who accepted my offerings and blessed me by putting a sacred thread, called a *mauli,* on my wrist and colored powder on my forehead, indicating I was protected by God.

In Haridwar, worshippers were preparing for the evening Aarti ceremony. Every twelve years, Haridwar is one of four sites that hosts a huge religious festival called Kumbh Mela. Tens of millions of people come from all over India—and the world—to participate and take a dip in the river. I was told it's total pandemonium.

Back in Delhi, I tried to make sense of this land of contrasts. The inviting aroma of spicy food would turn on a dime; the next moment, I'd be breathing in the gagging stench of decay. I tried to reconcile images of wealthy, upper-caste kids with those of the children who were eating spoiled food off the ground. Somehow, those children were equally full of laughter and curiosity.

There were opulent palaces, and families with barely a roof over their heads. I saw brilliant

Hindu priest at a mountain temple near Haridwar

Turbans can be nine yards long.

Opening My Cultural Lens

colors of women's saris, and sometimes naked—and always filthy—children. From the pristine air in India's protected jungles, to the choking fumes of pollution in the cities; and from quiet farmland to the maddening tangles of cars, motorcycles, trucks, busses, rickshaws, cattle, camels, goats, and pedestrians, it was a country of extremes.

Lower-caste family

Every time I started to wonder why in the world I was putting myself through the trials this trip involved, something extraordinary happened. I photographed the incredible Taj Mahal, caught a glimpse of tigers in the jungle, witnessed the spiritual sunset ritual on the Ganges, and was blessed by a Hindu priest on a mountain top. India is a country of opposites—a two-sided mirror.

I always come back from traveling overseas with a renewed appreciation for my everyday life, especially the countless freedoms I enjoy and try never to take for granted. While I treasure each and every moment of my experiences, I always look forward to returning home. The fact is, I am just plain lucky to have been born in America. I didn't earn this blessing; it came to me.

My eyes have seen first-hand the world's tremendous disparities, and I can't help but feel a responsibility to help address them. The reality of poverty is that one out of every five of the world's children, age six to eleven, does not attend school. The only way to break the cycle of poverty and end the exploitation of children is through education. When I came back from India, I searched for an organization that built schools in impoverished locations around the world. Right in my own Minnesota backyard was the Advocates for Human Rights.

Lo and behold, they were forming a committee to build a school in rural Nepal. A few years later, our dream was realized with the construction of the Sankhu-Palubari Community School, providing free education to kindergarteners through tenth graders in the Kathmandu Valley, close to where I had trekked. Today, at least half its students are girls in desperate need of a brighter future, away from child labor.

Bayon Temple, Anghor Wat

CAMBODIA & LAOS

When the World Stopped

On September 11, 2001, the world froze. The tragic attack on the World Trade Center and Pentagon shut down everything, especially travel. In America, people were scared to venture out. Flights were empty. Tourism stopped, yet security was at its peak. Because I travel alone, this also created a rare, safer-than-usual period in which to travel. So, off I went to Southeast Asia, anxious to see and learn more about Hindu and Buddhist societies.

    I began in Cambodia, which gained its independence from France in 1953. During that time, Saloth Sâr, a.k.a. Pol Pot, became a Buddhist monk, was educated in France, and then visited Yugoslavia where he was impressed by Marshal Josip Broz Tito, the communist revolutionary and dictator. Pol Pot (which stands for "politician potential") returned to Cambodia, joined the communist party, rose through the ranks, and became its leader in 1962. He and his followers took to the jungle to build a guerilla faction that became known as the Khmer Rouge.

Opening My Cultural Lens

In 1975, the Khmer Rouge seized power and began one of history's most horrific rampages. During the next four years, Pol Pot eliminated everyone he saw in his twisted mind as a threat. This included the educated class, political and business professionals, sixty thousand monks, and two million Cambodians—about a third of the population. The Khmer Rouge moved every person out of Phnom Penh and into 614 killing fields.

Unfathomably, Pol Pot convinced his followers to turn on their own families. No one was safe. After his soldiers killed the prisoners, he would kill his soldiers. He not only killed his own people; he tortured them first.

Pol Pot especially hated the Vietnamese, who deposed him in 1979. He died while in exile in western Cambodia in 1998. Cambodians believe he was poisoned.

Today, because Cambodia is so dense with jungle and still littered with millions of land mines, some places are not safe to visit.

Cambodia was Hindu until King Jayavarman VII (King J7) introduced Buddhism to the region in the twelfth century. King J7 built Angkor Thom, a huge complex that boasts more historic sites per mile than anywhere else in the world. The most famous of all the historic sites is Angkor Wat, the mother of all the temples, and one of the Ancient Wonders of the World. It's considered one of the world's most magnificent architectural achievements.

Buddhist woman offering incense

Hitching a ride, Phnom Penh

Cambodia & Laos

Angkor Wat

While many people are familiar with Angkor Wat, there are other extraordinary temples in this area. Bayon, for example, has fifty-four towers and 216 faces of King J7. Banteay Srei displays meticulous details carved from pink sandstone. My favorite, and one of the most interesting temples, is Ta Prohm, an ancient building now engulfed by huge roots from banyan and kapok trees.

Cambodia's main river is the Mekong, the fourth longest in the world, flowing for 2,500 miles. The other main water source is the Tonle

Ta Prohm, Siem Reap

Monks studying, Vientiane

Sap, a vast freshwater lake that is the heart of the country's agricultural and fishing industries.

Winding its way counterclockwise from Cambodia's northern border is Laos. A peaceful nation of easy-going people, Laos has sixty-eight distinct population groups. Not all are Buddhists; many are animists and shamanists, who believe in spirits and ritual animal sacrifice.

Vientiane, the capital and largest city, has some wonderful sites, including Wat Sisaket, home to the head of the Buddhist order of monks, and Pha That Luang, the most important religious building in Laos, which represents the different stages in Buddhist enlightenment from materialism to nothingness.

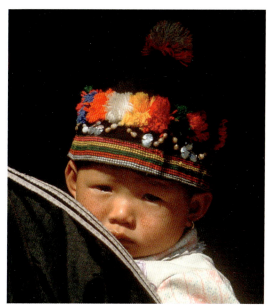

Pha That Luang   Hmong girl wearing a traditional hat

Even though the roads were dreadful, I was anxious to get up into the mountains to learn about the highland people, particularly the Hmong, many of whom have settled in Wisconsin and Minnesota, my backyard. Situated in the higher elevations of northeast Laos, Xieng Khouang is one of the areas where the Hmong live.

This area is also historic because it was one of the places in Laos most hit by American bombs during the Vietnam War. The Pathet Lao communist movement had its headquarters here. By the mid-'60s, US forces were pounding northern Laos in what was called the Secret War. More bombs were dropped on Laos during this time than in all of World War II in both Europe and the Pacific. And it all ended in failure when the communists took over in 1975, leaving the Hmong, who spent those nine years fighting for the United States, helpless at the mercy of the Pathet Lao. Many fled to Thailand; thousands died. I have Hmong friends who, along with their entire families, bravely immigrated to the United States during this period.

Opening My Cultural Lens

Keeping warm in the mountains of Xieng Khouang

My guide, named La, was from this mountainous part of Laos. I asked him about his Hmong family. La explained that to escape the bombings, most Lao either fled the country or lived in caves. One day, when La's mother was seven months pregnant with him, she needed to go find food and water for her family. She had six other children with her in the cave. She thought it was safe, but as she got outside, she was spotted and bombed. She was hit, losing both an arm and a leg. She was going to die. She screamed to a neighbor, also living in the cave, and begged him to help save her unborn child. The neighbor grabbed a knife, cut her open, and saved the child. This is how my guide entered the world. The name "La" means "last in family."

Health care and medical needs are handled by rituals. Before I came to Laos, I read Anne Fadiman's *The Spirit Catches You and You Fall Down*, a fascinating glimpse into this spiritual world. In Hmong tradition, when someone is ill, a medium is brought in. Sometimes it's a Shaman; always, it's a man. The family brings flowers, candles, and a chicken egg. The medium puts the peeled, hard-boiled egg in a bowl on top of some rice, inserts a coin into the yolk of the egg, then rubs the egg on the pain. After the ceremony, the medium checks to see if there is a black spot on the yolk. If there is, it means the sickness has been absorbed. If not, a chicken is brought in to be sacrificed. If the chicken doesn't cure the pain, then a pig is brought in. Neighbors come and watch and pray. Then, they eat the sacrificed animal.

A shortage of rural teachers hampers education.

To relieve fever, they put a glass into heated ashes then place the hot glass on the sick person's body, leaving circles but not a scar. Sometimes a person's soul is stolen by a *dab,* which Hmong traditionally believe is an evil spirit. Sometimes a soul gets lost and wanders around like a ghost. Sacrificing an animal is a way of bartering with the *dab*—to trade the animal's soul in exchange for the person's soul. And, when someone dies, the spirit, like a ghost, goes to a physical place before it's ready to be reincarnated. It is believed that the spirit of the dead person can invade the body of a live person because the spirit may want something and makes the living person sick before the dead person's spirit can move on.

From Xieng Khouang, I flew to Luang Prabang, the former capital and cultural center of Laos. Before the sun came up, I joined the local people to serve food to the monks, who queue up every morning to receive alms consisting of sticky rice. The monks only eat two meals a day, breakfast and lunch. I ended the day with a climb up to the top of Mount Phu Si to watch the sunset, all the while trying to absorb some of the phenomenal stories I had been told.

One of the highlights of the trip was being blessed by a Buddhist monk. My guide, Thong, arranged a private ceremony with the high monk of a temple on the edge of town. The monk sat before an altar. We were barefooted, sitting cross-legged on the floor. The high monk was told that I was from America. Since my visit was only a couple of weeks after 9/11, his prayers were directed at my safety. He prayed for nearly ten minutes, then placed spirit strings on my wrists and gave me a folded piece of cloth with some Buddhist scripture on it.

Monk at Mount Phu Si

The monk's blessing was intended to protect me from danger, to have a healthy body and soul, and to be happy all the time. I was to wear the bracelets for at least three days. My guide told me that this private blessing was rare and very special. Thong sat with me during the blessing and coached me through the ceremony, helping me to pay respect.

A young girl with hopes for the future

While time is the great healer, deep scars still exist as a result of the horrors of the Khmer Rouge in Cambodia and the Secret War in Laos. I was privileged to have met such extraordinary people who trusted me enough to share some of their most personal experiences to help me have a better understanding of their homeland, which today is enjoying peace.

Agriculture is the backbone of Rwanda's economy.

RWANDA

Weren't You Scared? Part One

I didn't know what to expect in Rwanda, a country that only a few years before my visit in 2011 had experienced one of the most horrific genocides in human history. I imagined an impoverished nation in total disarray. But to my surprise, I encountered a different country altogether, orderly and clean, with no outward signs of its recent conflict.

I began my trip in Kigali, the capital, where lots of new buildings and construction provided clear evidence Rwanda was moving forward. Still, it's impossible not to focus on what happened in 1994, when in less than one hundred days, nearly one million people of the Tutsi minority were systematically butchered by Hutu nationalists in one of history's most savage genocides.

Hundreds of thousands of children and young people were murdered in the 1994 genocide.

The violence erupted between two Rwandan ethnic groups of different social classes seeking power and economic dominance. Under Rwanda's Hutu president Juvénal Habyarimana, the Tutsis were stripped of much of their wealth and status. In retaliation, the Tutsis were planning to overthrow the president when he abruptly accepted a controversial peace treaty, granting the Tutsis a share of political power.

On April 6, 1994, Habyarimana's plane was shot down, an act that investigators concluded had been orchestrated by Hutu extremists opposed to the agreement who wanted to get rid of the president and eliminate all of Rwanda's Tutsis. Within twenty-four hours, government-led military death squads began torturing and slaughtering Tutsis and other political opponents, including moderate Hutu. The genocide immediately expanded from Kigali to the countryside.

A Uganda-based rebel army called the Rwandan Patriotic Front (RPF) marched into Rwanda and eventually into Kigali and began to seize government territory. By this time, hundreds of thousands had been murdered, and two million refugees, mostly Hutus, had fled Rwanda. Led by Paul Kagame, the RPF is credited with forging a peace deal in 1994.

A village outside Kigali

Kagame, a Tutsi, went on to become president. He has encouraged Hutus and Tutsis to live peacefully together, building national unity and boosting the country's economy. History will question why outside powers, including the United States and the United Nations, stood by and did nothing. Only time will tell if peace prevails.

As in much of northern Africa, Christianity and Islam are the two major religions in Rwanda. While tourism is a fast-growing sector, the economy is mostly based on agriculture. Farming in rural areas and in the mountains is extremely difficult. Workers, even kids, must carry heavy loads on their heads for long distances.

I had always wanted to track endangered gorillas in Rwanda, so I left Kigali and drove into the mountains. Tracking mountain gorillas is not easy. They're extremely well protected, and only a limited number of permits are issued to visit their habitat. Thanks to these preservation standards, the gorilla population is increasing.

I was assigned to a small team and briefed thoroughly on the strict rules. I stayed at a lodge that had no heat, just rubber hot water bottles that kept my bed welcoming and toasty as I fell asleep but were no comfort in the morning when I awoke to frosty air.

On the first of my two treks, we were looking for the Kwitonda, a group of twenty gorillas with three huge male silverbacks. We hiked through farm fields to the edge of the rainforest and then up the mountain—which, by the

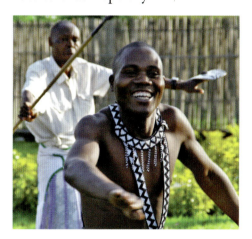

Dancers send off the trekkers.

way, had no paths. On the first day, we were very lucky. We had trekked just forty-five minutes into the forest when we reached a clearing. There, incredibly, I saw my first mountain gorilla. An adult male was sitting about twenty-five feet away, chewing on a bunch of bark. This big dude seemed oblivious that anyone had spotted him.

Gorillas are mostly vegetarians.

The average lifespan of a gorilla is thirty-five to forty years. An average male is about five and a half feet tall and weighs four hundred pounds. Each day he will eat fifty pounds of leaves, seeds, bark, and bamboo. The elder male is the leader. Gorillas are fully grown and ready to reproduce at ten to twelve years old. The oldest Kwitonda silverback was thirty-eight.

Female gorillas have the same gestation period as humans and have about three babies in their lifetime. But in gorilla culture, only the elder silverback is allowed to touch any of the females. If there are other males in the group, they hold out until the eldest dies, or they leave to form their own group.

Photography was challenging because the gorillas kept moving, and it was very dark under the canopy of the rainforest. I was standing against a bamboo tree, trying my best to take pictures of the group interacting, when I heard a rustling behind me. My naturalist guide heard it too and quietly said, "Just remain calm and don't move."

I did as instructed. A massive gorilla casually lumbered past me, brushing my arm and shoulder, knocking me off balance. My heart pounding, I closed my eyes, swallowed hard, and tried to remain still, wondering if my travel insurance had a gorilla clause. In that moment, this giant beast seemed as big as King Kong. It just sauntered past, paying me no attention. *Trust my guide,* I reminded myself, *and breathe.*

The following day, we tracked a new group of gorillas in a different area. Treks are measured by their degree of difficulty, and this second one was much tougher than the first. It was muddier and steeper, and I was tested.

In search of gorillas in the mountains

On this second trek, we stumbled for nearly three hours before spotting our first gorilla. Gorillas are very intelligent. They're shy, peaceful vegetarians. They also are generally quiet, that is, until they begin to communicate with each other with grunts, growls, and wild gestures, which include beating their chests, lunging, throwing objects, sticking out their tongues, and running sideways. It'll make your hair stand up straight if, all of a sudden, a giant silverback stands up and communicates right in front of you. Our guide told us to remain still and just watch them. I had a front-row seat for this show.

Gorillas are threatened by hunting and loss of habitat.

These treks were arduous but exhilarating. Adding to my unforgettable safari experiences in Africa, the Galápagos, and India, I was bolstering my profound regard for nature. I wondered as I left Rwanda, how its significance would influence my thinking—and my spirituality. I was eager to find out.

NICARAGUA

Weren't You Scared? Part Two

I learned early on that to begin to understand a culture, I needed to better familiarize myself with the historic events that shape their very societies. History is intriguing and instructional and often involves conflict and war. I've seen the aftermath of shattering tragedies and the resulting deep scars.

One such example occurred recently, in my adult lifetime, in Nicaragua, which I visited in 2012. As a point of reference, I was approaching thirty years old in the late '70s, when Nicaraguan dictator Anastasio Somoza was overthrown by the Sandinista National Liberation Front, which had ties to Cuba. By the 1980s, US-backed insurgents, the Contras, had begun a bloody guerilla warfare campaign to overthrow the new Sandinista government, which threatened American economic interests in Nicaragua.

The United States was not an innocent bystander, as it violated international law in its support and funding of the Contras, who attacked schools and hospitals and killed civilians. Tens of thousands died. The CIA actually wrote a training manual for the Contras called *Psychological Operations in Guerrilla Warfare*. The guerillas terrorized civilians, especially peasant farmers. America's involvement damaged its reputation.

Navigating the rainforest on the Papaturro River

Miskito woman in Tasbapauni

Caribbean beach near Bluefields

I spent most of my time on the remote, far eastern side of the country in the company of a guide named Julio. We talked about the Contra war, and I learned more about its effects on his family and his country. As we got to better know each other, Julio learned more about me, and that little grass grew under my traveling feet. He asked where I had been most recently, and I told him I had just returned from Rwanda, which in the 1990s suffered its own civil war and gruesome genocide.

I described Rwanda's biodiversity, rich with natural beauty, featuring stunning rainforests, volcanoes, and wildlife. I also told Julio one of the things I had always wanted to do in Rwanda was to track mountain gorillas. At some length, I explained that this required strenuous mountain hikes—all worthwhile, when at last, I spotted my first gorilla.

Julio's eyes grew as big as saucers, his expression a combination of shock, intrigue, and horror, as though he was thinking *you've got to be freaking crazy!*

He could hardly speak. "My God," he exclaimed. "Wasn't that dangerous? Weren't you scared?"

"Oh, no," I replied calmly. "If you just stand real still, they won't hurt you."

Julio's eyes narrowed, and he just stared at me. I suddenly realized he thought I was talking about guerrillas—as in rebel guerrillas—not big ape gorillas!

After he caught his breath, we both howled! *Geez,* I thought to myself, *and I'm in communications!*

Julio and his family must have lived in terror during that civil war and was likely feeling its impact years later. It's impossible to understand the long-lasting effect of war on a country and its people, and it's remarkable how the power of the hu-

Young boy, Solentiname Islands

man spirit can overcome immeasurable obstacles to find the courage, faith, and hope to envision a better future.

When I think of Latin Americans—their history, challenges, and hardships—I admire their cheerful and playful attitude. Perhaps it's the eclectic blend of their African, European, and Indigenous heritage that has influenced their pride and dignity. All I know is that this vibrant and dynamic culture is uniquely amazing.

GHANA

The Door of No Return

When I think back to my early education, I don't recall any comprehensive discussion about slavery. Blacks were a minority in my hometown, and there was not one Black person in my high school. The subject of slavery, as I recall, was all but glazed over in school, with students given only a basic overview of one of history's most gut-wrenching examples of human cruelty. But there are few issues more important to understand than the horrific trans-Atlantic slave trade, in which more than twelve million Africans were kidnapped, enslaved, tortured, and transported to the Americas.

Much of the slave trade originated in Western Africa, so in 2002, I headed to Ghana. I wanted—I needed—to know more.

The slave trade began in the late 1400s when Portugal claimed control over West Africa. To gain power and wealth, Portugal sent traders to West Africa to exchange manufactured goods such as cloth, metal, tobacco, liquor, and firearms for natural resources such as gold, ivory, and land. But it didn't take long for the Portuguese to figure out that *people* could be the biggest prize—men, women, and children could be sold and enslaved to manual work.

An ironic peaceful setting next to former slave castle

During the early seventeenth century, the Dutch joined in, followed by the British, bolstering a ruthless system of exchange called the "triangular trade." Here's how it worked: the Europeans brought goods to Africa. They traded those goods with African middlemen, who provided African captives to be taken across the Atlantic for sale in the Americas, where they were enslaved as farm laborers. Then, the Europeans returned to Europe loaded with sugar cane, tobacco, and cotton produced by slave labor. It was extremely profitable.

In Africa, trading was managed through a barter system. Africans captured natives to exchange for European goods. African middlemen raided villages, shackled inhabitants, and dragged them through the jungle to castles, where they were held in dungeons until they were sold and shipped. Greed and power were at the heart of this violent commercial enterprise.

At first, the slave hunt focused on criminals or those less desirable in African society. But the business became so big, entire families, including easier-to-capture women and children, were kidnapped. Families were separated. Human beings became cargo.

More than thirty thousand slaves were traded each year from the Elmina Castle.

On the Cape Coast, there are several notorious castles that were built as armed trading posts. But after the slave trade began, the fortresses became prisons. A prominent one I toured was the Elmina Castle, where prisoners were held before they were loaded onto ships headed for the Americas.

When the slaves first arrived at these castles, the middlemen began their bargaining. Typically, a male slave was traded for three guns and a woman for one. That was a small price because when sold in the Americas, the Europeans scored three times that price. The triangular trade was a gigantic money maker.

If families weren't separated upon capture, they were intentionally divided at the castles and confined to dungeons for as long as six weeks, waiting to be shipped. Regularly, women were raped by the authorities, including the local governors, then sent back to the dungeon. To say the conditions were unsanitary is an understatement. Trenches served as the sewage system. There was only a small hole in the ceiling for light. Captives slept on straw. Illness and disease were common. Countless died before they even got on the ship.

The slaves got their final look at their homeland as they passed through the Door of No Return, where they would be loaded on large cargo ships, branded, and chained for the five-week trip. The traders wanted to transport as many as possible, so they were stacked like sardines with hardly any room to breathe. The hot air reeked of vomit, waste, and death. Disease and malnutrition killed hundreds of thousands. Oftentimes, slaves were tortured, murdered, and thrown overboard, along with those who became so sick they were deemed worthless to a potential buyer at their destination.

Elmina Castle's "Door of No Return"

This atrocious trade lasted for more than four hundred years. During those centuries, 12.5 million human beings were kidnapped, and two million died. The global enterprise finally ended in January 1808 when the US Congress voted to abolish the slave trade, although slavery in America endured long after that.

A large portion of Ghana's population are farmers and fishermen. The South Atlantic coastline is dotted with fishing villages, where fish are smoked immediately because of the tropical heat and lack of refriger-

Commercial fishing, Gulf of Guinea

ation. Although the national language is English, more than seventy-five tribal languages are spoken. Twi, a dialect of the Akan, is the main native language.

About 25 percent of Ghanaians are Muslim. They have mostly settled in the north. The rest are Christian—very Christian. The missionaries did their jobs here. The faithful are enthusiastic about their religion and write bible passages and Christian phrases on their cars, boats, and homes . . . just about everywhere. Countless businesses are named in the Christian spirit: Christ is King Tires, Lord of Light Ventures, The Lord Cometh Beauty Salon, and Thank You Jesus Petro are just a few examples.

My guide and I headed north toward the central region. Thomas was

Ever-present Christian signage

his Western name, but children are often named after the day of the week in which the child was born. Born on a Sunday, Kwasi was his Akan name.

The potholed roads took us into the interior, which has a dense jungle and rich soils for agriculture. The people in this area may be very poor, but I quickly learned that their tight communities are exceptionally strong.

Noticeably, we passed a number of funerals. Thomas told me many funerals take place on Saturdays because it's a good weekend day to hold a celebration of life—oftentimes an all-nighter. In fact, Ghanaian funerals can last a week. People dress up in colorful traditional clothing, dance, sing, and party—all intended to bring joy to the dearly departed. The deceased is buried in an elaborate personalized coffin, often designed to represent the person's interests. Thomas said the coffins can be created to look like a football, boat, building, or an animal—anything goes. Music at funerals is top-notch, which is no surprise because Ghana is famous around the world for its folk, funk, jazz, and traditional highlife music.

It took us several hours to drive to Kumasi, the second-largest city in Ghana and the heart of the Ashanti Kingdom. The Ashanti are Ghana's dominant ethnic group. During the eighteenth century, the Ashanti conquered most of the territory. They traded Africans to the British in exchange for guns. As they prospered, the Ashanti culture flourished. They became famous for their craftsmanship and brightly colored kente cloth, a traditional Ashanti fabric that involves the intricate weaving of cloth, each color holding a different meaning, such as blue for peace, yellow for wealth, red for strength, etc. The iconic patterns are sewn together with symbolic designs intended as a means of communication.

A youngster wearing one of the many kenti designs

In the Ashanti Kingdom today, there are many chiefs from various villages, and dozens of tribal languages are spoken. Like many African cultures, great emphasis is placed on the villages' communal structure. Though the Ashanti are Christians, their communities also have a high priest, who, in some cases, is the village chief. I visited an Ashanti village near Kumasi. Thomas told me that the chief in this village was the guy through whom I gained access. A bribe was not out of the question. So, I came equipped with a bottle of schnapps as a gift and token of friendship, and I asked for permission to visit his shrine and village and to take pictures while I was there. It worked like magic. I joined the chief for cocktail hour.

Ashanti chief

We continued on to a village, home to the indigenous Akan people, who, in addition to Christianity, also believe in the *abosom*, which is a spirit of God. They believe the only way God speaks to them is through this spirit, which is typically embodied in nature. The shrine is where the spirit lives and only manifests itself through a medium called an *Okomfo*, the high priest who becomes possessed by the spirit and speaks for it. The Okomfo, who also assumes the position of a medicine man, is the most important person in the community.

Akan village elder

Throughout this trip, I had so much to process. I only had begun to learn about Ghana, and particularly about the slave trade—the most inhumane forced migration in history. And I had only scratched the surface about the profound and enduring impact slavery has had on my own country.

Curious kids

Today, Ghanaians are attempting to better understand this chapter in their history by sharing experiences, respecting their ancestors, and embracing their heritage. Every year on March 25, the International Day of Remembrance of the Victims of Slavery and the Transatlantic Slave Trade, global citizens honor those who suffered and died.

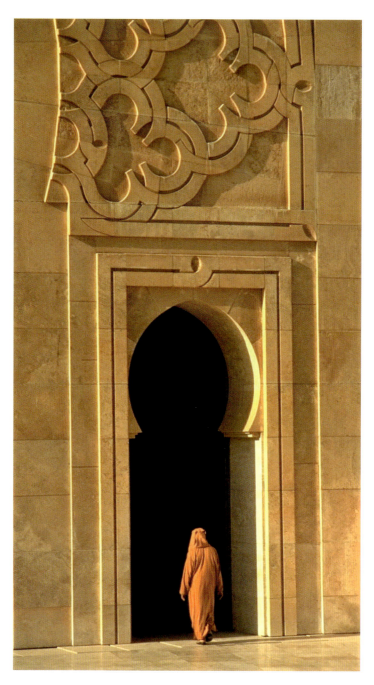

A mosque's impressive entrance

MOROCCO

Rock the Kasbah

It was a stroke of luck that I visited Morocco during the ninth month of the Muslim calendar at Ramadan, the period when the faithful believe God revealed to Mohammed the Islamic truths that are written in the Koran. Muslims steadfastly observe this holy period, fasting for thirty days.

My devout guide, Ahmed, gave me a crash course in Islam. He felt the best place to start our journey was in Casablanca, whose name—White House—comes from the city's many white buildings. Our first stop would set the stage for my entire trip. We went to the Hassan II Mosque, the third-largest and most expensive mosque in the world, after Medina and Mecca.

Tallest minaret in the world, Hassan II Mosque, Casablanca

Splashed by the waves of the Atlantic, the grand mosque is so large that twenty thousand Muslims can pray inside, and another eighty thousand can worship in its massive courtyard. During Ramadan in Morocco, non-Muslims are not allowed inside any mosque; no exceptions.

Morocco is blessed with the Rif and Atlas Mountains ranges, two coastlines, and the infinite Sahara Desert, and I couldn't wait to get out of the big city and into the countryside. We headed east to Rabat, taking back roads that revealed soft colors and hypnotizing hillsides. The Romans dominated the area until the Berbers settled in 429 BC. When Islam was introduced by the Arabs in the seventh century, the Berbers embraced it.

Rolling hillsides, Rabat

One of the best examples of Moroccan architecture is the kasbah, a small town within a fortress that served as the residence of the local sultan or a wealthy family. These citadels were a refuge for nomadic tribes and merchants traveling along the Silk Road who needed a safe place to stay.

While kasbahs are unique to Morocco, so are *riads*, traditional Moroccan homes. In Meknes, one of the oldest cities in the country, I stayed in a historic riad. It had no heat nor hot water. Only Arabic was spoken, and only traditional Moroccan food was served. Meknes is famous because it was the home of Moulay Ismail, a cold-blooded, merciless sultan. He had a harem of five hundred wives and concubines, from which he had hundreds of children. He was a heinous tyrant who strangled his daughters at birth

Blue Kasbah of the Udayas

and sliced off the limbs of sons who disobeyed him. In an effort to intimidate everyone, he once displayed seven hundred heads on the walls. It worked.

Just east of Meknes is Fès. I spent an entire day in the medina, or old town, where four hundred thousand people live, work, and worship in more than three hundred mosques. The weather that day was dreadful, so it was a good time to be inside the medina. Very narrow walkways led to shops, markets, and businesses of any imagination, including a fascinating tannery, which stunk to high heaven. I was cold, soaking wet, and had just spent the day gallivanting through mud and donkey dung, which was on more of me than just my boots. I started to stink too.

On our long drives, Ahmed and I had interesting conversations. Most marriages are pre-arranged, he explained. The whole clan can get involved, although the girl's mother is the first to approve and give the green light. We talked a lot about religion and its role in local culture. "In today's Morocco, progressive women are in conflict with Muslim tradition," he said, "as they interpret the Koran differently than men."

Opening My Cultural Lens

I asked if he had been to Mecca, something required of a Muslim in their lifetime as part of the Five Pillars of Islam. He had not yet, but he told me it took his grandfather one year to ride a mule to Mecca and another year to return. I'm still not sure what was more amazing, that it took a year or that he rode a mule. In any event, the man was faithful.

Archways in local medina

As we drove, we'd stop at some of the *souqs*, lively outdoor markets usually held on Tuesdays or Wednesdays in virtually every town. It was a great place to photograph people who'd come on their donkeys from the mountains and neighboring villages to sell and to shop.

We set out on what I thought would be a relaxing all-day trip south through the Atlas Mountains, but it didn't turn out quite as expected. First came the rain, then the sleet, which then turned to snow, which fell as we traversed skinny, curving mountain roads with no shoulder. We did not have four-wheel drive. Fishtailing down the slippery mountain roads was not my idea of a good time. As the weather worsened, we started seeing downed trees, flooded and closed roads, and detours. My anxiety level was well past nail-biting, especially because Ahmed kept saying, "inshallah"—God willing. Thanks, Ahmed, but not helpful.

Eventually, on dry land and in warmer temperatures, we drove through the Ziz Valley where Ahmed introduced me to a family he knew. The clan we visited was a large extended family whose ancestors had lived in this home for hundreds of years. After a cup of tea and a cookie, the father and mother kindly showed me around. Their kasbah had stone and dirt floors. There was no electricity or plumbing, but no one seemed to mind. I chased around the alleys and walkways with some little kids. It's a maze inside, and it was easy to get lost—the perfect place to play hide and seek.

Kasbah, Ziz Valley

Marrakech has many historic buildings. The landmark Koutoubia Mosque, with its 252-foot-tall minaret, was built by a sultan at the beginning of Morocco's first great dynasty in the eleventh century. Its minbar, where the Imam addresses worshippers during Friday prayers, is one of the most exquisite examples of woodwork in Islamic art.

Back in the day, the decadent El Badi Palace was built with magnificent details, including being covered in white Italian marble. Then the ruthless Moulay Ismail (remember him?) went to work. Over a twelve-year period, the tyrant stripped all the grand buildings in Marrakech of many of their irreplaceable materials in order to build his own palace in Meknes. One of the buildings he plundered was El Badi. The palace took twenty-five years to build, but sadly at the hands of Moulay, just twelve years to destroy. Today, only remnants can be seen, but the beautiful minbar from the Koutoubia Mosque is the highlight of the ruin.

The red clay buildings of Marrakech

Finally, we arrived—inshallah—in the southern part of Morocco, gateway to another item on my bucket list. I had long yearned to photograph the sunrise on the Sahara Desert. The farther I ventured into the desert, the better the photographs would be. I was in for quite a trip.

The outing began at 2:15 a.m. on a crystal-clear night. We drove into the desert for more than two hours, passing Berber tents with families tucked inside, sound asleep. The stars were gigantic. Further out, there were no tents. There was nothing.

Finally, I met up with Wasim. (At least that's the name I gave the friendly camel who was to give me a lift to the dunes.) The name means Handsome, and this camel seemed happy to see me.

In the middle of the night in the desert, the temperature was in the low thirties. My camel whisperer, a Berber named Mohammed, put a heavy blanket over my shoulders. I tried desperately to hold onto it while clenching an ice-cold metal saddle bar and the long-lens camera dangling around my neck. Camels are uncomfortable to ride in the best of times, and my back spasmed for days.

After an hour and not all that far from the then-troubled Algerian border, Mohammed finally pointed to some tall dunes that he felt would provide the vantage I was after. It was still dark. We left Wasim, who just stood there waiting. There was nothing to tie a camel to, and frankly, nowhere for him to drift off to anyway. We began to climb. It was a workout. Our feet sank deep into the soft sand, knocking us off balance. Mohammed and I hung onto each other as we staggered up the dunes.

Upon reaching the top and breathing in the crisp cold air, we gasped at the billions of giant stars that were simply out of this world—pun intended. It's impossible to describe how quiet it was. Absolute silence! Nothing moved. No wind, no insects, just complete stillness. I had never experienced total silence until that moment. There have been a few times in my life that I would describe as spiritual. This was one of them.

My footsteps to the top

As the sky began to lighten, I got a first glimpse of the vast landscape. There was nothing in sight but sand—pure, unblemished sand. My anticipation was growing by the second.

Mohammed, who spoke no English, was soon to become my camera grip. In those days, I was shooting film, and I knew in this instance I had precious little time between rolls to reload. I showed Mohammed, who had never seen the inside of a camera, how to remove a roll of film, place it in its own little canister, then remove a new roll of film from an unopened canister and load it into the camera. His newfound talents proved most helpful. We made every second count.

The sun finally broke, casting long brown shadows over deep orange sand. It was the exact moment to photograph: before the sun peeked over the horizon, becoming stark and bright and washing out the shadows that had cast mesmerizing waves in the sand. It was the exact moment to capture the peaks and valleys that shaped wonderful, dramatic, geometric patterns. I was shooting like there was no tomorrow, with Mohammed, my efficient grip, at my side.

The sun rose quickly, and it was time to make our way down the giant dunes. At the bottom, good old Wasim was waiting faithfully to give me a ride back to the truck. In the daylight, I got a better look at the desert flats and how they evolved from gravel-like sand into smoother sand, then into flawless dunes. With nothing in sight but desert, I couldn't figure out how the driver knew where in the world he was going. What landmarks could he possibly be following? He was a Berber. He just knew.

The Siq, Petra

JORDAN & LEBANON

I Wonder What They're Saying About Me Now

It was bound to happen sometime. I arrived in Jordan with no luggage. Amman was formerly called Philadelphia, which I feared is where they might have sent my bags. My guide's name was Firas. He was a friendly (and tall, dark, and handsome) young guy who, I learned over the course of my visit, had about ten girlfriends.

Missing luggage notwithstanding, I was eager to head south to one of the world's most famous archaeological sites, the lost city of Petra. On our drive, Firas and I tried to figure out how my bags might catch up with me.

Lined with miles of beautiful olive groves, the Jordan Valley is located on the northern end of the Great Rift Valley. On a clear day, you can see the West Bank of Israel and the Dead Sea. We stopped at Mount Nebo, where it is believed that Moses lived his last days and died. We continued south along the Dead Sea—where Jesus was baptized and John the Baptist lived.

Soon we traded our car for a 4x4 to drive into the Arabian desert. We traveled through Wadi Rum, called the Valley of the Moon because of its prehistoric red sands, rugged cliffs, and rocky mountains, and we passed the Seven Pillars of Wisdom made famous by T. E. Lawrence, who pitched camp here.

Wadi Rum

Along the way, we saw many nomadic Bedouin camps. I visited one, taking off my shoes before entering. I sat down on a rug cross-legged with my toes not showing nor pointing outward. As I enjoyed my hosts' coffee, the head of the household explained that Bedouin life is very simple. They need goats and camels for milk, meat, and skins. The tents are owned by the commune, not by an individual.

Bedouin camp, Arabian Desert

Early on the morning of day six, Firas received word that my luggage had finally arrived. *Inshallah!* His plan was to drop me off with a local guide, Omar, whom he knew very well, then drive three hours to the Amman airport and meet me back in Petra later in the day. I was grateful Jordan was not such a large country that this errand was impossible. Off he went.

Omar introduced me to an older Bedouin fellow who wore the traditional red and white keffiyeh headdress held in place with an agal. The man, well into his '80s, explained that in Petra, there are three thousand limestone caves where many Bedouin lived. Omar told me he also used to live in such a cave. He liked the peace and quiet and being close to nature. In the mid-'80s, the government moved families from the caves into other housing to help preserve the sites. While it was difficult imagining Omar living in a cave, I kept thinking there was no way Firas could. After all, how could he date ten girls while living in a cave?

Keffiyehs are headscarfs that protect men from sun and sand.

Red cliffs and sandstone hills dominate Petra, the "Rose-Red City," which UNESCO describes as "one of the most precious cultural properties of man's cultural heritage." Two thousand years ago, some thirty thousand people lived here. Temples, tombs, and theaters were all a part of this famous ancient city, whose entrance is a dramatic ravine called the Siq.

I crept through the mile-long Siq, a narrow gorge lined with three-hundred-foot-tall rocks, to get my first look at the most remarkable of all of Petra's rock-carved buildings: Al Khazneh, or The Treasury. While its purpose is unclear, some believe the 130-foot-high structure, with its Greco-Roman façade, began as a temple with tombs where the Nabataeans stashed gold and jewels they traded or stole.

The Treasury, crown jewel of Petra

I reunited with Firas, and with my bags in the trunk, we headed north back to Amman. At this point, having returned twice this week from Amman, he must have been tired of this road, but he never said a word. Nursing a sore back, I asked if there was somewhere to stop to get a massage. There were only small towns along the route. But Firas, a Muslim, knew of a place that would be, as he said, "okay." It was not exactly a rave review, but as I keep saying, I trust my guides.

Let another cultural *faux pas* unfold.

It was very late in the afternoon and was getting dark as we entered the "massage parlor." The lobby was bleak and harshly lit by several bright fluorescent ceiling lights. Three large guys with a lot of facial hair were sitting in folding chairs pushed against a wall, smoking something strong, and watching a TV perched high on a shelf. My entrance drew their attention away from the evening news. I stood there, smiling and nodding at them as Firas exchanged a few words with the masseuse named Ahmad. I was the only customer. I quickly surmised this was not a place where women got massages.

Ahmad, who spoke little English, pointed to the dressing room—a storage closet divided by a pastel-flowered shower curtain. (The juxtaposition was precious.) I looked at Firas just to make sure this was, you know, "okay." He nodded. The looks on the faces of the guys in the folding chairs were memorable. It's hard to say what they were thinking, but it probably ranged from *Oh geez, you gotta be kidding me*, to *Can't wait to tell the rest of the boys this story*.

I was in a pickle: my Muslim guide said, *okay*, the

Muslim masseuse thought, *why not*, and I always try to be as respectful as I can of other cultures—especially their religions. Yet, here I was: a woman in a Muslim country, with a Muslim masseuse in a place where women are not allowed. In the end, I figured if they're okay, I'm okay.

So, I popped out of the dressing room like a Jack-in-a Box. I had on nothing but a robe. The guys in the folding chairs didn't know where to look—the TV? Their shoes? Just not at me.

Ahmad ushered me into a private room. This room was also divided by a curtain—an out-of-place plaid fabric that matched nothing else. There was no chitchat from this guy, but I got quite the massage. I'm certain he was apprehensive. And he must have been wondering what the guys in the lobby were whispering. If only I understood Arabic.

After I redressed in the little closet with the pastel-flowered shower curtain, I paid and tipped Ahmad for his services—and for his discomfort—very generously. The three men in the folding chairs were still in the lobby. I nodded respectfully, not expecting a response. Nothing else was said, at least until after I left.

The next morning when I woke up with remarkably diminished back pain, I wondered if getting a massage back home would ever be the same.

Feeling refreshed, I was ready to continue on to my next stop, Lebanon.

The Bible calls Lebanon the land of milk and honey, and from snow-capped mountains to the fertile Bekaa Valley, this small country is indeed gifted. Its well-preserved history stars the Greeks, Romans, Arabs, European crusaders, Egyptians, Ottomans, and the Phoenicians, who, by the way, are thought to have created the first real alphabet.

Bekaa Valley

Fast forward to the twentieth century.

It wasn't long after colonial Lebanon finally got its independence from France in 1946 that the Arab nationalist movement sparked instability. In 1958, Egypt and Syria formed the United Arab Republic, but Lebanon wouldn't join, which peeved its Arab neighbors. Lebanon's recent history includes the Six-Day War with Israel and the Arab region in 1967; the 15-Year War with Israel that began in 1975; the Syrian intervention that began in 1976; and the 2005 assassination of Prime Minister Rafik al-Hariri, which took place just a month before my visit.

Against this backdrop of turmoil, war, and destruction, Lebanon proudly celebrates its independence. Half the population is from outside the country, including numerous Palestinians who've come there to live and work. The country is majority Muslim and more than a third Christian.

The Sunnis and Shia are two different sects of Islam. When Muhammad died, Islam was divided over who should succeed him. Two sects resulted because Muhammad had no heir. The difference between the two has to do with who they each believe is Mohammed's caliph (or successor). Like Christianity or any other religion, the Shia and Sunnis include many different secular Islamic groups—some are moderate; others are very conservative.

Sunni and Shia friends

In Lebanon, Shia and Sunnis typically hold separate services at the mosque. When the call to prayer is announced, the Sunnis go to the mosque first. Fifteen minutes later, the Shia enter. However, on some occasions (such as a national protest), both sects have been known to pray together, alongside Christians, as a show of unity.

It wasn't always this way. During the civil war that began in 1975, Beirut's infamous Green Line was drawn, dividing the Christian east from the Muslim west. While the fighting is over, the Green Line has left psychological, as well as physical, scars. Yet, often called "the city that would not die," Beirut is resilient. After fifteen years of war, reconstruction was ubiquitous. Whether restoring what was nearly obliterated during the wars, or excavating the country's earlier history, Beirut is always under construction.

Because Lebanon is so small, it was efficient to start out in Beirut; the vibrant renaissance capital once called the Paris of the Middle East. Situated on the Mediterranean Sea, the city is a sophisticated liberal center of cultural innovation. Lebanon, by the way, has a remarkable literacy rate of 90 percent, the highest in the Middle East. Students today are taught Arabic,

French, and English. French influence is also represented in Lebanon's art, food, fashion, and nightlife.

Beirut rests on a peninsula on the Mediterranean.

While there were checkpoints all over the city, it was still possible to explore its historic and religious sites, many of which date back three thousand years. Calmed by a warm salty Mediterranean breeze, I enjoyed a walk on the corniche, a seafront promenade that also offered great people-watching. New high-rise apartments, office buildings, restaurants, and shops were evidence of how the city is trying to re-establish itself as the crown jewel of the Middle East.

Using Beirut as my base, I set out to see the ancient sites along the sea, including the seven-thousand-year-old Byblos, the oldest continuously inhabited city in the world; Tyre, the Phoenician settlement that fought off Alexander the Great; and the four-thousand-year-old town of Sidon, where Greek, Roman, and Byzantine archaeological remains are all protected.

I then crossed over the ten-thousand-foot Qurnat al-Sawdā mountain, the highest peak in the Middle East, to get to the Bekaa Valley. The Bekaa is home to Baalbek and Aanjar, two of the most classical ruins in the country. Baalbek was inhabited as early as 9,000 BC and is one of the most important Roman sites in the entire Middle East.

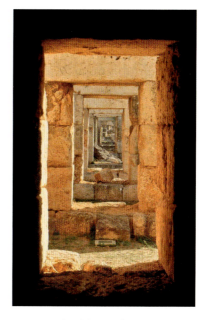

Tyre's historical sites

Opening My Cultural Lens

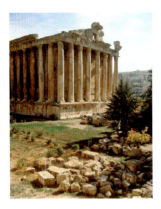

Ancient Roman ruins, Baalbek   Armenian settlement, Aanjar

Aanjar is an Armenian town that was founded by refugees fleeing genocide in Turkey during the first century. Archaeologists discovered that the vast settlement was actually a thriving city with a Roman layout dating back to the early days of Islam. It was once a major market on the Silk Road.

In the heart of the cities, souqs are filled with spicy aromas and eager vendors. I visited one on Thanksgiving. For decades, my travels took me out of the country at this time of year, and I dearly missed my family's scrumptious turkey dinners. In Lebanon, where Thanksgiving was just another Thursday, I ventured out to have some authentic shawarma, one of the Middle East's most popular street foods. Everywhere I went, seasoned meat roasted on vertical spits in storefronts, seducing diners. Throughout the Middle East, I've enjoyed chicken and beef shawarma, so it was an unexpected surprise on this day to find turkey slowly turning on the rotisserie.

With a full stomach, I continued north to the well-preserved city of Tripoli in the Qadisha Valley. It is called the Holy Valley because there are eighteen monasteries, including the monastery of Saint Anthony. But before heading home, I also wanted to see the Cedars of Lebanon. Located in the famous forest mentioned in the Old Testament, some of the ancient trees are upward of two thousand years old.

Not only does this small nation boast numerous ethno-religious groups, but it also tests how Christians, Shia, and Sunni Muslims all live—and govern—together. Remarkably, this power-sharing model is in Lebanon's very constitution, which says the president will be a Maronite Christian, the prime minister a Sunni Muslim, and the speaker of the parliament a Shia Muslim.

Qozhaya Monastery, Qadisha Valley

Lebanon's intentional plurality makes this country stand out. In addition to its application in government, this diversity is reflected in its architecture, education, and arts throughout society. With all that Lebanon has endured and continues to face, it seems to me that its multiculturalism is the glue to its unity and its greatest strength moving forward.

NAMIBIA

Do You Live as Well in Your Land?

With my backpack loaded with camera gear, I headed out on an adventure I had been anticipating for a long time: an exceptional chance to visit some of the world's most ancient tribes.

On a recent trip to South Africa, I learned about the nation's history of discrimination and apartheid, and how European settlers dominated the indigenous groups. Namibia was part of South Africa at the time and also suffered from a century of colonialism. During the ruthless reign of the Germans, Namibia's tribes fought for their independence. But in 1904, an uprising by the Herero people was met with genocide. Germany issued an "extermination order," and about 60 percent of the Herero population was wiped out.

After World War II, Germany was forced to turn Namibia over to South Africa, which continued its apartheid and white-settlement policy. But in 1990, international pressure helped Namibia finally gain its independence from South Africa.

Although the official language is English, Afrikaans is spoken in most homes. My guide, Charles, was an expert in Namibian culture and also had a great eye for photography. We were about to meet some phenomenal indigenous people who would give us a rare glance into a window of our own past.

Bushmen have lived in the Kalahari for more than twenty thousand years.

We began in Windhoek, the capital, and headed toward Tsumkwe (in Boesmanland), which is located in the Kalahari in Namibia's northeast. Because we were out in the bush, we traveled on rugged and rutted dirt roads. There was not much to see other than meerkats and gigantic termite mounds.

In this remote territory, my accommodations were basic. I stayed in small buildings in small villages. My bed was narrow, and we had no electricity. Fortunately, the temperatures, though warm, were not too hot. Getting out into the bush was the only way I could spend time with some of the most unforgettable indigenous people on the planet.

Traditional headdress

The Saan, or Bushmen, as they're often called, are one of the oldest continuous cultures on earth. The first village I visited was one large extended family of about fifty. Kunta was the headman, or chief, and also the medicine man. The Bushmen are known for their knowledge of "the bush," and they relate to their history through dance and storytelling. Known as the "Original People of Africa," they still practice traditional hunting and gathering.

They also have a very distinctive language that involves clicks, which Kunta tried to teach me. It's not easy. Here's a couple of examples in his tribal language:

- *ii-ame* means water: Click on both sides of the inside of your cheeks while simultaneously saying, *ah'-may*.

- *ii-aisa* means foot: Click softly on the top of your mouth while simultaneously saying *eye'-sah*.

Though I think they appreciated my effort to attempt clicking, I remained the butt of their jokes. Kunta wasn't done with me yet. Together with his brother-in-law Kaece, Kunta tried to teach me how to hunt and trap small animals and birds. I went off into the bush, following two otherwise naked men wearing only loincloths.

Hunting with Kunta and Kaece

First, we gathered poison to use on the arrows. Buried in the sand are poisonous grubs. The Bushmen spread the deadly juice of these insects on the tips of their darts. Next, from scratch, we made rope from a plant. The rope would be used to build the trap. Twigs are then placed in the ground, and a branch is bent with a piece of fruit or a seed on the end as bait. When an animal or bird steps inside to grab the bait, the rope snaps around its neck. Then it's time for dinner. But first, we had to build a fire to cook the dinner. With the patience of Kunta and Kaece, this city girl passed all the tests.

For ten thousand years, the Bushmen have been considered one of the world's most resourceful people, living completely off the land. By age twelve, a young Bushman will be able to identify and know the purpose of two hundred plants. By age sixteen, that number will double. In the bush, everything has a purpose.

The Bushmen's spirituality focuses on the Sky God, whose mystical insights teach joy, especially through vibrant dancing and laughter. They also believe in two "chiefs" or gods. The "Good God" lives in the east and created all things, and the "Bad God" lives in the west and causes evil, sickness, and death. The Bushmen are aware that outsiders who are unfamiliar with their spirituality have not been prepared to understand their practices.

I was about to see this for myself.

When we returned to the village after a day of hunting and trapping, we learned a young man from a neighboring village had come to seek help from Kunta, who is also the witch doctor. The sick man was hurting from head to toe and didn't know what was wrong. A small child from the village was also ill. Kunta went to work.

He put on his ankle bracelets and smoked some kind of tobacco. The women sat in a circle clapping and chanting while Kunta—with help from Kaece—danced ecstatically around them, trying to work himself into a trance. Once in a higher state of mind, he attempted to communicate with his ancestors, who would give him strength and advice.

I could not believe what I was witnessing.

Namibia

A trance dance connects a healer with ancestors.

The more he danced, the closer he got to the trance. In time, Kunta's actions became more physical and anxious. The women in the circle supported him with more and more clapping and chanting. In a spiritual frenzy, Kunta would hold the ill child, then stand up and dance. At one point, he ran into the bush to spit out evil spirits. Then, he did the same thing with the sick man. Kunta held the man's face, neck, and chest, attempting to draw out the evil spirits and release the sickness.

Kunta reaching an altered state of consciousness

After leaving the village, Charles and I could not stop talking about the mind-boggling healing ceremony. Our conversation was followed by long periods of silence as we both reflected on what we had just experienced. Witnessing the extraordinary, deep connection Kunta had with the Sky God was, well, out of this world. And the patients were indeed on their way to feeling better.

We continued on our drive—again on rutted, dusty roads—to Oshakati in northern Namibia, home of the Ovambo people. Ovambo homesteads are known as kraals, which have a circular living space with labyrinth-like passages intended to confuse the evil spirits.

Ovambo woman fishing in a shallow pond

The men were out with the cattle and goats. The women do all the heavy lifting. They take care of the children, cook, and see to all the planting and farming. Ovambo men can have many wives and outlive the women because the women have much harder lives.

As I travel around the world, I experience countless patriarchal societies that, for thousands of years, have continued to maintain systems that are unfair and disparaging to girls and women. Confronting these behaviors is unavoidable as a global traveler. While it bothers me a great deal to learn of these injustices, it's not appropriate for me to challenge their ways; I experience these cultures as their "guest." I am there to learn.

One of the indigenous groups in Africa I found most fascinating was the Himba. We headed to the Kunene River in the very remote northwest corner of the country, on the border of Angola. The semi-nomadic Himba are descendants of the Herero and are one of the most unique tribal cultures on earth. Because they're so isolated, no one really knows how many Himba are left. Most don't send their kids to school because their lives are centered on goats and cattle. Their spirituality is based on communication with their ancestors.

Many live deep in the northern region's Zebra Mountains. With the help of Charles and another local guide to translate, a Himba family allowed me to enter their village. The Himba observe the traditions of their ancestors. Their beliefs provide contact between the living and the dead, which keeps the ancestors happy. Their kraal is very simple and includes a main family room for sleeping. They sleep on straw and leaves with a hide or a blanket on the ground.

Himba are known for their ochre-colored skin. When a woman reaches puberty, she will cover her body with ochre, which is her makeup and reflects her beauty. She will scrape the red ochre rocks into a powder and mix it with butter and a bit of mint for an improved scent. She will not use water to wash it off, but she will steam the mud in incense to cleanse herself and to smell fresh.

Married women wear a small headpiece on top of their braided hair, topped with a crown of goat ears as well as a metal-studded plate that hangs down their back. Himba women also wear a heavy cross-shaped necklace and other jewelry made from copper, ostrich shells, and woven reeds. Ankle bracelets are made of wire that's heated and shaped. Men make them for women to protect them from snake bites.

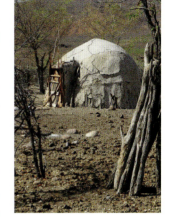

Kraal

Braided hair covered with red ochre

While Himba men can take multiple wives, the head of the family I visited had only one. It's less expensive, he explained. He had very long hair—braided and tied up in a turban—to indicate he was married. When a man's father dies, the man will wear his hair down for one year, then tie it up again. Our host used a little spear to scoop up his snuff, which is made from tobacco, fire ash, and some potent herbs. My guide laughed and said he also uses the spear to get at an itch inside his turbaned head.

Head of household

Cattle and goats constitute wealth. The territory of each clan has to be large enough to move herds long distances, chasing pastures freshened by rains. Along their way, the men construct rough camps as temporary housing, but they always return to their home village. When I was there, it had been critically dry, and the father was about to set out on a long journey to check on his cattle, which had already been moved a hundred kilometers away for pasture. It would take him a week to make the grueling trip.

A traditional ceremony of the Himba is performed on all boys and girls as a rite of passage into adulthood. The father will take a hard, sharp stick and knock out the child's bottom four teeth. Male relatives hold

Friendly bat over my bed

the child down as the ritual takes place. Then they heat up a metal spear until it is red hot and put the tip on the wound to stop the bleeding. Next, they place mopane leaves on the wound, as the tannin of the plant will stop the blood from clotting. Finally, they will file the top two teeth into points. I will never complain about going to the dentist again.

Displaying filed teeth

Himba headman in Opuwo

Charles and I continued along the Angola border near Opuwo until we reached a village that was home to a large, extended family. The headman had been napping when we arrived, resting the side of his head on a narrow wooden "pillow" about two inches wide and six inches tall. He insisted it was comfortable. He gave me his pillow as a souvenir to try at home. My impression was correct. It's not comfortable.

The translator told me Himba boys shave their heads while the girls braid their hair back to front. When the girls get their second period, they will braid them front to back. Marriage is arranged by families when boys are in their late teens and girls are even younger. At the wedding, the daughter's family presents the groom's family with some cows. Women will give birth in the bush, where other women in the village will help.

Opening My Cultural Lens

I visited with a group of women who, when learning that I was still single with no children, sprouted unforgettable looks of confusion and disbelief. To them (and likely to a lot of others), I'm an odd one. I always find it amusing. I wonder how my translators describe my life to those whose customs are so different.

At first, the children in these villages were very shy and didn't know what to make of me. They kept their distance. Then, soon, they were all over me, laughing and singing and wanting to hold my hands. Charles was getting such a kick out of these otherwise-timid kids.

Shy kids

As we drove farther south toward Damaraland, the hillsides began to change color. Sands from the Atlantic's Skeleton Coast have pushed eastward to create a rugged semi-desert landscape. Here, we visited the Herero. The women wear long, multi-colored dresses layered with different fabrics. Their unique headwear resembles bull's horns, symbolizing the significance of the cattle in their lives. Everyone was anxiously awaiting the rains that would sustain the herds.

The horned headdress shows respect for cattle.

For all the years I've traveled around the world, I continue to be astounded at the many indigenous people perfectly content with living the simple life. Often, they don't seem to have the stress and worry of so-called modern societies. Their spiritually enriched lives are peaceful and playful, centered on enduring traditions in supportive village communities.

But even in these remote areas, change is expected. Older generations try to preserve their history, language, and rituals while younger generations may slowly drift away, living half in and half out of westernization.

Fearing further development, the Himba are retreating deeper into isolated areas. Because of this, they may survive longer than most tribal cultures. Yet, they need miles and miles of space for their herds to graze. Without goats and cattle, my translator said, the Himba will die. But in the meantime, they are content.

As one Himba elder explained, "Our life is good. We have no fighting, no crime, no hunger, and no hatred. We are satisfied. Do you live as well in your land?"

Good question.

The Western Wall

ISRAEL

In the Cradle of Humankind

If you think for a moment that by going to Israel, you will leave with a better understanding of its religious, historical, and political complexity—good luck. No two people are likely to see this country the same way. My favorite expression, told to me by a Jewish elder, sums it up. "Put two Jews in a room, you'll get three stories."

Knowing that no one will ever understand this astonishing place, my guide, Irit, provided a primer to help me begin to navigate Israel's tangled history, traditions, and multidimensional cultures. She was exceptionally knowledgeable, and she loved to laugh—a great combination that made for a most memorable trip.

Israel has been a Roman Province, a Crusader Kingdom, and a domain of Egypt, Turkey, and Britain. Just some of its notable rulers and citizens include Hercules, Alexander the Great, Cleopatra, Napoleon, Abraham, Moses, Jesus, and Muhammad. Therein lies the historical and spiritual significance of Israel.

Opening My Cultural Lens

My introduction began in Jerusalem, a holy city for Judaism, Christianity, and Islam. A great many of those who visit are on a pilgrimage, tracing their religious roots. Admittedly, I was not one of them. While the base of my spirituality was formed in Christianity, like virtually everyone I grew up with, I'm not religious so much as I am spiritual. That said, I was fascinated by those who are enthusiastic about their respective religious interests.

Jerusalem was built on seven mountains by King David and is divided into the Old City, East Jerusalem, and West Jerusalem. It's the Old City that most people recognize. The walled city is so small that I could walk around it in an afternoon.

Jerusalem, home to the world's three largest religions

First constructed by Süleyman the Magnificent, the Old City has eight gates and houses four distinct quarters: Jewish, Muslim, Christian, and Armenian. Among the Old City's 220 historic treasures is the Temple Mount, home to the Dome of the Rock, the oldest Islamic monument and one of the city's most important symbols. The significance of the Temple Mount is its recognition by Judaism, Islam, and Christianity. For Jews, it's where Abraham prepared to sacrifice his son to prove his faith; for Muslims, it's where Muhammad ascended heavenward to take his place alongside Allah; and for Christians, it's where Jesus spent the last days of his ministry.

Visiting the Western Wall was not what I expected. I thought it would be a more somber place, but it was not. Yes, there were many who came there to pray and to grieve, but it also was packed with lively activity. The Western Wall, considered the holiest place for Jews to pray, is the only remaining part of the retaining wall that once surrounded the Temple Mount. The Romans destroyed the Second Temple in 70 AD.

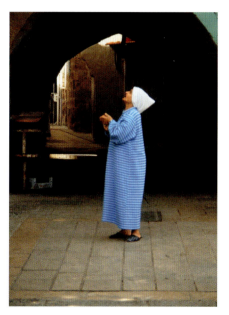
Woman in Old City, Jerusalem

Reading from the Torah

Scraps of paper containing prayers of the faithful are stuffed into the wall's crevices. It's commonly called the Wailing Wall because many Jews weep over the destruction of the temple at this site.

When I was there, Orthodox law prohibited women from praying freely at the wall. In 2016, a government decision created a new space that allows women to pray alongside men.

Right next to those who are there to mourn and to pray at the Western Wall, there are festive public bar mitzvahs and bat mitzvahs. I enjoyed photographing these ceremonies. Dozens of Jewish families from all over the world gathered at the celebrations, which were all taking place at the same time. I couldn't tell one family from another, as the events seemed to merge together to become one big party. Following each ceremony, the shofar (or ram's horn) was sounded, and hundreds of people danced and sang.

Festive bar and bat mitzvahs at the Western Wall

It's impossible to digest the significance of the countless historic and sacred sites. I recall how remarkable it was to stand overlooking the walls of the Old City at the Mount of Olives, where Jesus, on the back of a donkey, made his triumphant entry into Jerusalem. It is where Christians believe Jesus ascended to heaven. About seventy thousand Jews are buried there; their graves marked with white stones.

Mount of Olives

One of the most gut-wrenching experiences is to pay respects at the Mount Herzl (the Mount of Remembrance) at the Yad Vashem Holocaust History Museum. This chilling exhibit is dedicated to the 1.5 million children who were killed by the Nazis during World War II. A dark underground memorial features hundreds of mirrors that reflect the light from four candles. Each tiny light honors the souls of the children who perished.

Israel

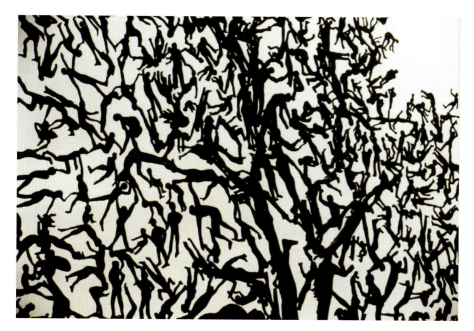

Yad Vashem Holocaust History Museum

Before leaving Jerusalem, I wanted to learn more about the Ultra-Orthodox Jews who live in a restricted community called Me'a she'arim. Residents here are often offended by non-Ultra-Orthodox Jews, and entering their community is discouraged. I was warned, if I tried to get out of the car, they might spit on me. And, on Shabbat, I'd be forbidden from entering. If I tried, I might be stoned. I stayed in the car.

Me'a she'arim, a community for Ultra-Orthodox Jews

Leaving Jerusalem, we drove through the Judean desert toward the Jordan River. The Dead Sea Scrolls were found here in 1947, in the caves of Qumran. One day, a Bedouin shepherd boy looking for a stray goat found the texts. They were inside old earthenware jars written on parchment and leather. The Dead Sea Scrolls are a significant collection of ancient religious manuscripts, many containing biblical texts.

Close by, on a mesa in the hills above the Dead Sea, is Masada. After Judea became a province of the Roman Empire, hundreds of Jewish freedom fighters took refuge on top of the mesa. King Herod sent fifteen thousand Romans to conquer them. The Jews in Masada had to decide between slavery or suicide. When the Romans finally reached the top, only one woman and her children were found alive. She said that ten men were selected to kill all the others, with one last man killing himself. Masada has become a national symbol for Israel.

Masada

I wanted to visit areas controlled by the Palestinians, so we drove north through the West Bank. After the Six-Day War in 1967, Israel got control of the territory on the West Bank of the Jordan River, but both the Israelis and Palestinians claim rights to the area. Under the terms of a 1994 peace accord, the Palestinians agreed to recognize Israel. In exchange, a number of cities would be turned over to the Palestinians. Some of these cities under Palestinian security include Bethlehem, Jericho, Ramallah, Nablus, and Hebron. At the last minute, my guide got word that it was not safe to travel there, so the excursion was scratched. I was disappointed but reminded how important it is to have a local guide with ears on the ground.

Israel

On the Sea of Galilee, I stayed at a kibbutz, an agrarian collective. Agriculture isn't as profitable as it once was, so kibbutz communities have found other ways to make money, including opening guesthouses and museums. One example is on the Jordan River, where Christian pilgrims come to be baptized. I watched as a group of Japanese pilgrims dressed in white robes were submerged in the holy water.

Baptism in the holy Jordan River

The next morning, Irit realized her vehicle needed some maintenance. We were on one side of the Sea of Galilee, and her mechanic was on the other. She thought it might be interesting for me to spend the time it would take to get the car fixed by experiencing a boat ride across the sea, one of Israel's holy sites, as well as the country's largest freshwater lake. The ride would only take a couple of hours. It was a beautiful day, so it sounded like a swell plan. At the dock we learned there were lots of boat tours scheduled but, unfortunately, no available space. We were about to leave when we found a group from America that had chartered a boat and graciously allowed me to hitch a ride to the other side of the lake. Perfect timing.

I got on the boat and sat out of the way toward the back so I wouldn't intrude on the private charter, which I soon learned was a group of thirty or so evangelical Southern Baptists. They paid me no mind, chatting with each other in anticipation of their journey to trace Jesus' footsteps. The Sea of Galilee, after all, is

Opening My Cultural Lens

said to be where Jesus had performed miracles, including walking on water. (Earlier that day, I learned there actually was a "Walking on the Water" tour, though I don't know what it entailed.)

As we pushed away from the dock, a senior member of the group led the pilgrims in prayer, an invocation that seemed to have no end. We had been on our way for about a half hour when that first meditation concluded, but the pilgrims only became more invigorated. More prayers followed. The pilgrims jumped to their feet and praised the Lord while speaking in tongues.

This is the part of the story when I must admit that while I consider myself a spiritual person, I was fearful the pilgrims would encourage me to rise up and join their ceremony. I grew up in a very passive and subdued religious environment, so this excitement was quite new to me, and I did not know how to react. As any introverted Lake Wobegon Lutheran, I shrunk into my seat, lowered my head and shoulders, and stared at my feet, praying—yes, praying—the pilgrims would not see me nor call on me. Thankfully, their passions were building to such a crescendo they were completely unaware that behind them I was withdrawing in terror.

The cruise continued. We were more than an hour out, literally in the middle of the Sea of Galilee, when the prayers finally wound down. I took a deep breath and tried to focus on the cool breeze on my face. I was relieved it was finally over.

Then, without explanation, the captain turned off the motor, stopping the boat in the middle of the sea. On cue, the minister sprang up and began his emotionally charged sermon. His fervor—reliving the life of Jesus where he preached the gospel—continued for another hour, spurring the pilgrims to yet a higher, altered state of enlightenment. Tears flowed. Euphoria.

The sermon finally came to an end. The pilgrims were exhausted, and so was I. We were still in the middle of the lake, only halfway home. The captain started the engine, and we cruised in silence the rest of the way to the dock.

I had somehow conserved enough energy to bolt through the crowd so I could disembark first. (I couldn't help thinking of George Costanza in the *Seinfeld* episode where he frantically raced to the exit past all the women and children after someone yelled "fire.") Scampering the length of the boat without breaking stride, I shouted a genuine "Thanks for the ride" to the group leader and, like a skilled quarterback, lateralled a generous donation to the minister. As I catapulted onto the dock, I took off searching for Irit, who could tell by the look on my face that a story would follow.

One of the most fascinating religious groups here is the Druze, established in Egypt about one thousand years ago. The number of Druze is limited because no one can "convert" any longer. To be a Druze, you must be a descendant of a Druze mother and father. They believe in Allah, but they also believe in reincarnation. They study the Koran, as well as the Old and New Testaments.

In Haifa, Israel's largest harbor, I was introduced to yet another faith group—the Baha'i religion. Haifa rises from the sea to Mount Carmel, where I visited the Baha'i temple and walked around its famous and impeccably lavish gardens, taking in the sweet air of the floral blossoms. The Baha'i faith is a combination of Buddhism, Christianity, and Islam. They believe in one God, and in the unity of all religions and human beings, and they promote peace.

I needed so much more time to continue to learn about this complicated place where history and religion are mixed, stirred, and consumed, though maybe not truly blended. Israel is a collision of cultures where

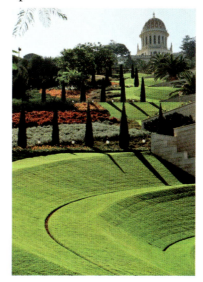

Baha'i Temple, Haifa

different people, religions, and ideas ram into one another. Israel is further complicated because everyone seems to have a different interpretation of the scriptures, and everyone believes their faith is the truth.

Tragically, the ongoing conflict between Israelis and Palestinians sees no end. Most recently, in 2021, another outbreak of violence killed and injured innocent families and children, destroyed homes and property, and fed human rights abuses. Israel continues to seize and occupy land, which prevents the development of critical housing projects and infrastructures for millions of Palestinians.

The Israelis and the Palestinians each indisputably claim the West Bank and Gaza Strip. Also, both sides not only recognize Jerusalem as a holy place but as their capital. Most experts believe a two-state solution, which would create an independent Palestine alongside Israel, is the only path toward peace, but the same experts believe that achievement is next to impossible. Neither side is willing to budge.

So, as the chasm between the Israelis and the Palestinians deepens, the fighting ensues, directly affecting those who cannot afford

Golan Heights, a strategic military location in Eastern Israel

Israel

further suffering. As both sides continue to battle, many fear a full-blown regional war could erupt, pitting multiple countries, including Arab nations, against one another. How would the international community respond? And what role would the United States play?

Israel, to me, is complex and baffling, with each historic event influencing the next. Still, there's no place like it. Look at the present, and you'll find the past; look at the past, and you'll find the future. Stir in new religions, add countless wars, mix in new prophets and lots of kings, and you have an ever-changing region that defies comprehension.

You bet I'd like to go back there someday.

Mongolia is known as the "Eternal Blue Heaven."

MONGOLIA

What's on Tap?

Mongolia may not be on most folk's bucket list, but it sure was on mine. I had so many reasons to see this rugged untouched country—an exotic adventure that had been on my list of "musts" for years. I had heard so much about its nomadic culture, huge mountain ranges, breathtaking landscapes, and stunning Gobi Desert. Its nomadic lifestyle is fascinating. And Mongolia is a photographer's dream. Furthermore, I've continued to be interested in Buddhist countries—particularly the Tibetan model of Buddhism—which is practiced by the majority of people here.

Mongolia is the size of western Europe. Tragically, when the Soviets took over Mongolia in 1939, most of the monasteries were destroyed, and the monks were either killed

Traditional deel clothing

or exiled to isolated parts of the country. When the Soviet Union unraveled in 1990, so did its tight grip on Mongolia. Unfortunately, right after the collapse of communism, lacking Soviet support, Mongolia fell into a deep recession. The country finally stabilized after its state-run economy was reformed.

Elderly woman in Ulaanbaatar, home to half of the country's population

During my visit in 2009, Mongolia's capital city, Ulaanbaatar, was in the process of trying to redesign itself after decades of Soviet dominance. After their precious freedoms of speech, religion, assembly, and press were restored, the country was in a frenzy of infrastructure rebuilding. Old, bleak, Soviet-style buildings were being replaced with colorful and more architecturally interesting designs. Construction affected every block of the city, and traffic was mayhem.

I was met by my guide Ishbaljir, or Ishee for short. We had the same silly sense of humor; we clicked, which made this trip so much fun.

Joyful children

Freedom was still new to Mongolians, and they were digging it. Previously, the Soviets banned most media. Ishee told me pop culture didn't exist in those dark days, and American TV shows were finally making their way into Mongolian living rooms.

While Mongolia is one of the oldest countries in the world, much of its history revolves around a twelfth-century guy by the name of Genghis Khan—or Chinggis Khan, as the Mongolians prefer. Chinggis was the founder of the Mongol Nation and is the most significant person in its history. This notorious warrior ruled the largest land empire in history; he's regarded as a brilliant strategist. He began his reign by killing off all the clan leaders and bringing the survivors into his fold, creating an army of two hundred thousand soldiers, which soon became a million. With only nine generals, over the next twenty-five years, he conquered half the world.

Chinggis practiced psychological warfare, forcing his prisoners to serve in the front line, and somehow, getting opposing tribes that fought each other to serve with him. To those who surrendered, he promised protection, religious freedom, lower taxes, and other benefits.

His spiritual guidance came from what he called the "Eternal Blue Heaven." Today, Mongolians revere the Eternal Blue Heaven as a sign of their tenacity and spirit.

Bactrian camel

Chinggis Khan may be known to the world as a ruthless conqueror, but he's regarded by most Mongolians as the greatest leader and lawmaker in history. Others agree: in 1995, the *Washington Post* named him "Man of the Millennium."

I couldn't wait to get out of hectic Ulaanbaatar and into the Gobi Desert. As I traveled overland (without roads), my accommodations abruptly changed. I stayed in a different *ger* each night. Nomads developed circular structures (which the Soviets called yurts) to adapt to the cold, wind, and sun. A ger's entrance consists of a framed wooden door always facing south so the sun can keep the inside warm. The men sit on the west side and women on the east, where they also cook.

Opening My Cultural Lens

Gers, dwellings of nomadic people

Inside a cozy ger

Because of the nomadic roots of this culture, hospitality is at its center: the more guests, the merrier. Ger doors are never locked. If no one's home, guests just walk in, light up the fire, and make tea. Payment is never made, and in fact, is considered an insult. Guests are always offered salt milk tea, and *boortsog*, which are deep-fried cookies with a few candies thrown in.

Literally seeking greener pastures, most nomads move two to three times each year. Some, however, must move every month. Therefore, they can dismantle a ger in less than an hour. Gers are light, so they can be transported on the backs of a couple of camels—or on a pickup truck if the owner is lucky enough to borrow one.

Nomadic people are known for their hospitality.

One night we arrived at a camp of about eight gers plus a little building where we ate. A small group of Germans was also staying there. In typical German fashion—I would know, I'm from Milwaukee— they had brought a keg of beer— "Chinggis" beer, to be exact. It didn't take but a second for Ishee, our driver, and me to crash their kegger. We didn't really know what they were celebrating; we just saw the beer.

236

We spent a great deal of time in the desert, which occupies the lower third of the country. One of the highlights was Khongoryn Els, where the desert sands are pushed up against the hills. They're called the "Singing Sands" because of the movement of the wind over the shifting sands. These massive dunes are over 2,600 feet high, seven miles wide, and sixty-two miles long.

Navigating steep dunes is much easier by camel, specifically the two-humped Bactrian camel, nomadic herders breed for meat, milk, wool, and transportation. I'm not wild about riding camels, but the sand was too soft, loose, and deep to hike, so this little blossom took the ride.

It took well over an hour to reach the top where I'd get the best view for my photos. What a view it was! The untouched dunes, Khongoryn River, green grasslands, steppes, and plateaus were exhilarating. I was thrilled no one else was in sight—just dunes that seemingly had no end.

Mongolians honor shamanistic spirits on the high points of the landscape with *ovoos*. Like Buddhist chortens, they are piles of stones but have been decorated with blue silk strands. Ishee and I always tossed a handful of stones onto the pile and observed the tradition of walking clockwise three times around the ovoo to honor the spirits.

The year before I was there, Mongolia was victim to a devastating *dzud*, a die-off of animals caused by

Sacred Ovoo

summer drought, followed by a severe winter. Thousands of families lost their entire flocks. Five million animals died from starvation. We visited my driver's family, whose father had a flock of about eight hundred sheep and fifty horses. He lost more than five hundred sheep to the dzud, he told Ishee and me over salt milk tea and sour curds.

Families here are resourceful and efficient. Everything has its place and is easily packed up when the time comes to relocate. Most nomads have a motorbike and a little solar panel. These supply energy to a car battery, which provides enough juice for a stereo, TV, and small refrigerator.

Ishee and I trekked in an area called the Flaming Cliffs, a gorgeous landscape of red sands and hills, where, in the 1920s, explorer Roy Chapman Andrews discovered the world's first-known dinosaur eggs.

Flaming Cliffs

It was only September, but winter was coming fast. Because of the country's mile-high altitude, temperatures would soon change from ninety degrees to negative fifty. One night, for example, the temperature dropped from eighty-eight degrees to twenty-eight degrees, freezing our water.

I was particularly interested in visiting Karakorum, the capital of the Mongol Empire from 1206 to 1368. At its peak, under the reign of Chinggis Khan, the domain covered twelve million contiguous square miles (from Japan to Hungary and about the size of Africa!), making it the largest land empire in history. Here at Karakorum, I attended a ceremony at a four-hundred-year-old Buddhist monastery—a vivid example of the revival of this religion in the country. We entered a colorful prayer hall, the architecture rich with bold colors and symbols representing aspects of the Buddha's life.

Young monks, Karakorum monastery   Celebrating religious freedom

First, two monks climbed up a platform to announce the call to prayer. They blew into large shells. They gathered outside the hall and then slowly filed inside to begin the ceremony, which included chanting, candle lighting, gongs, and horns. I was not allowed to take photos inside, but I sat across from the monks as they recited and repeated verses from scripture.

It was fitting to close my trip with this very meaningful experience. It had only been a few years since Mongolians had been able to openly practice their religion, and that significance was not lost on their faces.

Over and over again, as I travel to places that do not share the same freedoms we enjoy in America, I feel a deep gratitude and appreciation for my homeland. Liberties are fragile, and they're not guaranteed. I will never, ever take them for granted. A truth underscored by my next trip—to "the Stans" in Central Asia.

THE STANS OF CENTRAL ASIA

Stranger in a Strange Land

When I imagined Kazakhstan, Kyrgyzstan, Tajikistan, Turkmenistan, and Uzbekistan—I kept hearing the fictional character Borat's accent, like a song stuck in my head that I couldn't turn off. The Stans, as they are called, are located in Central Asia between Russia, Afghanistan, Iran, and China. I was curious to see how these countries had changed since the collapse of the Soviet bloc. In 2014, I decided to find out.

I began in Ashgabat, the capital of Turkmenistan, which sits right on the Iranian border. With a ton of brand-new buildings and corporate offices, Ashgabat was completely unexpected. After a starched hello from my government-issued guide, I was informed that photographing certain things, especially military and sensitive government buildings, was strictly prohibited. If I tried, it would land me in jail. Welcome to Turkmenistan.

A one-party police state, Turkmenistan is often called the "North Korea of Central Asia." It's one of the world's most repressive countries, ranking second from last in its lack of press freedom—only North Korea is considered worse. Getting a visa took more than eight months. It required me to get a letter of invitation and numerous backup documents that I had to carry with me as I went through countless—and I mean, countless—checkpoints.

Man wearing traditional embroidered cap

Turkmenistan is situated right in the middle of a precarious geopolitical region. While determined to be a neutral country, it is loaded with oil and natural gas that it exports mainly to Russia, which turns around and exports it to Europe.

Perhaps because it experienced the Soviets' state-enforced atheism, Turkmenistan is very leery of anyone imposing any religion on the country. It's particularly vehement about making sure radical Islam does not reach its borders, including extremists from Iran and the Taliban from Afghanistan. The fear is the suppressed economy and society might make radical Islam more appealing to those who have fewer options. Keeping potential problems at bay also keeps the West out of its hair.

Just how strict are the border controls? Upon arrival, my passport was sent off to some government authority, and my whereabouts were monitored. I was informed before I left the States that I should expect my hotel room to be bugged, and I was required to have a guide at my side at all times. No roaming around for this curiosity-seeker.

The Turkmen people are liberal Sunni Muslims who also hold traditional animist beliefs. After the Bolshevik revolution in 1917, Turkmenistan became part of the USSR. As the Soviet Union collapsed, Turkmenistan's communist party leader, a guy named Niyazov, was determined to hold on to power. Niyazov was an eccentric, egocentric dictator who appointed *himself* president for life. He even gave himself a legal name, which he made everyone call him: "The Great Turkmenbashi," which meant the "Leader of the Turkmen." He made himself the center of an omnipresent personality cult. It gets better.

Colorful folk headdress

Niyazov erected golden monuments of himself, including one gold statue in a Superman cape that rotates to face the sun. The president's photo was omnipresent and mandatorily plastered everywhere. Taxi drivers had to have his photo on their dashboards. Niyazov banned gold teeth and insisted television hosts couldn't wear makeup. (I was told he couldn't tell the males from the females, though I'm not sure what that meant.) He also decreed how to refer to people as they aged: "childhood" lasted until age thirteen, "adolescence" until twenty-five, "youth" until thirty-seven and, since he was particularly sensitive about aging, "youth" did not become "old" until after eighty-five. It was reassuring to learn I was not old.

This guy was so full of himself that he actually renamed the weeks and months of the year after himself and his family members. Niyazov renamed the word for bread after his mother. He banned the circus, ballet, and listening to music in cars. People were expected to take spiritual guidance from a book he wrote entitled *Ruhnama*, a collection of his thoughts about Turkmen life. (I can see *Saturday Night Live*'s Phil Hartman now: "Deep Thoughts by Turkmenbashi.") Reading the book was required.

Opening My Cultural Lens

The megalomaniac also spent billions on grandiose projects, all while cutting social welfare. His theme was "People, Nation, Me." He wanted to be worshipped as a god. Speak out against him, and you'd end up in prison. He abolished the Internet, free press, and other liberties, and was condemned by the West for violating human rights.

Back in 1948, in less than a minute, a nine-point earthquake leveled Ashgabat and killed two-thirds of the population. The city was rebuilt in drab Soviet-style architecture. In 1985, when Niyazov became leader of the communist party of Turkmenistan, he began to rebuild Ashgabat using its endless oil and gas reserves to finance ostentatious construction projects. The city streets are lined with hundreds of white marble palaces and gold domes. Many of its buildings have distinctive shapes: a five-star hotel is shaped like a teardrop; the main library is designed like an open book; the gas company looks like a lighter; and the Health Ministry is affectionately said to resemble a female body part. I'll let you guess.

Health Ministry, Ashgabat

Niyazov died unexpectedly in 2006. Turkmenistan reverted to a normal calendar, but even after a new president, constitution, and democratic elections, little changed. Freedom of the press, religion, movement and expression were not restored, and those who push back are brutally punished. Its people remain oppressed, and the country continues to be one of the most corrupt in the world. They trust no one.

So, yes, I was under surveillance.

Niyazov's supporters credit him for transforming Turkmenistan from a poor Soviet republic into a self-sufficient economy. He also built up agriculture from nothing and provided his people with clean water, free gas, and electricity.

Turkmenistan is 80 percent desert. We headed north into it to see some of the (approved) spiritual sites. People make pilgrimages to numerous archaeological sites to worship ancestors who are buried there. The Turkmen are very traditional people. They walk around the holy burial sites three times counterclockwise as they pray for good luck. They leave offerings as wishes to Allah.

Pilgrimages are an important way of life in Turkmenistan. And just like many traditions, families afterward will gather for a big dinner.

A family on pilgrimage

They lay out the carpet (literally, a bunch of huge carpets) and have a big potluck. Grandparents, aunts, uncles, children—they all get together. They first sacrifice a lamb, then feast for hours. Families insisted I join them for dinner, so I took off my shoes and sat on the floor as they piled food in front of me. They couldn't wait for me to try the lamb stew. The men sat with the elder of the family and ate separately from the women and children.

This experience was the other side of life here—lovely, friendly, curious people who could not have been kinder. In Ashgabat, I was monitored under a watchful eye. But out here in the desert, it was far

Opening My Cultural Lens

Welcomed at a community dinner

more relaxed. I came unprepared (without gifts), but that didn't stop *them* from sending me off with parting gifts. They thought it was a good idea to give me a bunch of things they somehow felt I needed, including, not in any particular order, a bag of sugar cubes, cookies, a loaf of bread, a ladle, a towel, and some hosiery. Hosiery . . . that was a first.

I thanked my new friends for their hospitality and continued north to Uzbekistan. This has to be one of the most secure border crossings in the world. Getting into North Korea was easier.

Here at Dashoguz, I parted from my guide and checked in at the first military station only to be directed to the next checkpoint. I smiled at the official, picked up my bags, held my documents in my hand, and proceeded to the next station. And the next. I went through six, maybe seven, checkpoints. I thought I was finally across, but the border has a kind of a "DMZ" they call "no man's land." I had to walk outside about one hundred yards, dragging my luggage over gravel, to yet another building with the actual border in the middle of the building. There, I went through three more checks. *Patient, just be patient,* I reminded myself, grinding my teeth. *This is a government customs border crossing.*

I exited the other side of the building, now in Uzbekistan, hoping I could put away my passport. Instead, I had to drag my bags over another hundred yards of gravel to yet another checkpoint. Déjà vu all over again. I wondered if I was on the Stan's version of *Candid Camera*. No one spoke English, which was not helpful because I had to fill out forms at most of the checkpoints. I didn't know what I was filling out: name, numbers, reason for visiting? I had no idea. Stranger still—because none of the officials read English, they had no clue what I wrote! It was the most bizarre experience.

This whole process took well over two hours. I was worn out. Finally, as I approached a barbed wire fence that separated the security area from visitors, there was my trusty new Uzbek guide patiently waiting for me. Relief.

Few Uzbeks benefit from minerals, oil, and gas wealth.

Uzbekistan is about the same size as Turkmenistan but with more than six times the population. It does not have oil and gas wealth. It was the heart of the Great Silk Road, but its history also includes ruthless leaders, including Chinggis Khan, who, back in the day, ravaged the area.

It also has a poor human rights record and is pretty much closed to foreign journalists. Freedoms, while better than Turkmenistan, are limited. The government takes better care of its people but will not allow assembling or protesting that could lead to trouble.

Another interesting tidbit is that while the United States denounces many of Uzbekistan's policies and actions, it stays away from sanctions because Uzbekistan allows the Americans to have a strategic airbase on the eastern side of its border with Afghanistan. Like Turkmenistan, it fiercely controls its bor-

Education is free for all children.

ders to keep out radical Islam and the Taliban. It will take no chances of having any extremists threaten to overthrow its government.

We drove to Khiva, located in the southwest part of the country. In the past, it was a major pit stop for gruesome journeys across the desert. Built in the twelfth century, Khiva was a notorious slave market known for its barbaric cruelty. Caravans of tribal slaves rounded up from the desert were traded there for three centuries. In spite of this past, people here are proud of their traditions and of the impeccably preserved heritage sites that show off their ancient history.

Opening My Cultural Lens

Elderly man visiting mosque

Mosaics of Kalyan Mosque

We followed the Turkmenistan border for hours. We were on a lonely highway mostly used by truckers bringing freight to Afghanistan and Tajikistan. The road was punctuated only by military checkpoints. We finally arrived in Bukhara, which is considered the country's holiest city. In the ninth and tenth centuries, Bukhara became the center of an intellectual, religious, and commercial renaissance. But the Soviets distrusted Islam and outlawed its practice. From 1932 to 1936, Stalin closed mosques, arrested mullahs, and turned places of worship into museums, dance halls, factories, and warehouses. Atheism was promoted, and Muslims were forced to worship privately at home.

Courtyard, Lyabi House, Bukhara

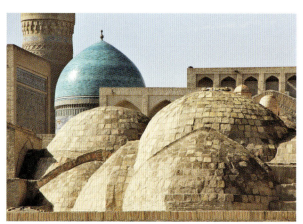
Toqi Zargaron Trading Dome, Bukhara

Samarqand is Uzbekistan's most glorious city, with stunning architecture, bazaars, and parks. Hundreds of years ago, it was already being built into a cosmopolitan city—until Chinggis Khan obliterated it. Then along came Timur, who began a nine-year rampage through the region. He stole riches and captured artisans. Then Timur built

The Stans of Central Asia

Lyuli woman resting at mosque   Tila Karl Madrasa in the Registan Square, Samarqand

his capital, Samarqand. He turned the city into a showcase of treasures, featuring some of the richest tilework in the Muslim world.

The Stans illustrate how countries change over time. They have faced geopolitical, cultural, and religious crossroads that their rulers—from Chinggis to Timur to Niyazov—decided how to navigate. Partly because of their precarious juxtapositions, they undoubtedly will continue to face critical choices.

While my guide in Turkmenistan was more formal toward me—nice, but always making sure I didn't cause him any trouble—my guide in Uzbekistan was more conversational and open. He seemed quite happy with his life. However, on our last day, I asked him what he'd like for his future. He didn't have to think to answer. "Freedom."

Girl at Umayyad Mosque, Damascus

SYRIA

Hospitality of Strangers

Syria is on my mind all the time. I spent three weeks there in 2009 when life was quiet and peaceful—before the recent civil war that brought the country to its knees, and before I saw the destruction of sites I still can't believe I was blessed enough to have visited.

My guide, Ahmad, and I began in Damascus, Syria's capital and largest city. He was a mature, low-key guy whose grasp of history, politics, and religion was beyond his young age. We spent hours on end talking about his homeland. He was not only a terrific source of information, but he also became my friend. Today, as the war continues, I wonder about Ahmad, his whereabouts, and his circumstance.

Damascus competes for the title of being the oldest continuously inhabited city in the world, with archives going back 3000 BC. It was fought over by the likes of King David of Israel and Alexander the Great. It is where biblical Cain killed brother Abel.

Nearly 95 percent of Syria's population is Muslim. The Umayyad Mosque, the city's centerpiece and Islam's first Great Mosque, is one of Islam's holiest sites, ranking only behind Mecca and Medina. When visiting Umayyad (and all mosques), I covered my arms and legs, usually wearing an abaya (which is like a cloak), and a hijab, which is a headscarf worn by most Syrian women as a testament to their faith. Some women prefer head coverings with only a narrow slit for their eyes. Others totally cover their faces with a thin black fabric, allowing them to see and breathe easier while showing extreme respect and virtue for their husbands.

As the first few days went by, Ahmad and I needed to get to know one another, and I needed him to trust me. Because with that trust came deeper conversations about life today. With more than three weeks to spend together, each day brought new insight. In Islamic society, traditional values and discriminatory laws deprive women of many basic legal and social rights. For example, one in four Syrian women suffers from domestic violence; honor crimes accuse women of immorality; and marital rape is not a crime. Syrian society places the burden of sexual morality on women, who must obey their husbands if they want any financial support.

Schoolboys, Aleppo

Holy Day

Syria

We traveled north through Maalula, where a priest recited the Lord's Prayer in Aramaic, the language of Jesus, which is still spoken here today. We continued to the Roman city of Apamea, and then to Aleppo, which once was the meeting point of several key trading routes.

Farther north on the Turkish border is St. Simeon. The Byzantine ruins are named after Simeon, who, at a very young age, took on a monastic life. Quite the eccentric, he retreated to a cave in the hills. When people found out about his pious life, many came to seek his blessing. But Simeon couldn't stand to be around other people, so he erected some pillars and spent forty years living on top of them! He'd preach from up there but would never speak to women, including his own mother.

The hospitality of strangers is built into the lives of those in the Middle East, a place where nomadic Bedouin have, for centuries, needed the kindness of others, as they traveled from one location to another trading, or searching for food, water, better pastures, or safer conditions.

Young Bedouin child

Goat shepherd, Raqqa

For years, I, too, have enjoyed that kindness throughout the Middle East, but perhaps my most memorable experiences took place in Syria. One day, Ahmad and I were driving along the Euphrates River, which runs from Turkey through Syria to Iraq. The

Opening My Cultural Lens

river is the source of political tension, as all three of these countries compete for the use of its waters for irrigation and power. We drove from Raqqa to Dayr al-Zawr, an area that just a few years later would be controlled by ISIS.

It was Holy Week, which precedes hajj, the annual pilgrimage to Mecca. Because so many Muslims want to go, people must apply. In Syria alone, twenty thousand Muslims are granted permits each year. Those who do not make the trip spend this week feasting with family. Those that can afford it buy and sacrifice a sheep. A third of the sheep goes to the farmer, a third goes to the buyer, and the final third to the poor. Hundreds of thousands of sheep are slaughtered over a two-day period. Being a part of this ceremony is unavoidable.

On the roadside, we passed a Holy Week gathering of about seventy-five family members. Curious, I asked Ahmad if there might be the slightest chance I could get a photo—just one quick shot. As I mentioned before, almost everywhere I go, local people are quite curious about me, this older woman traveling alone. My guide approached the elder of the family, who took one look at me and nodded.

I timidly walked up to the elder, Karam, and greeted him by saying, *"as-salamu alaykum,"* which means "may peace be upon you." Karam began to show me around his spacious yard when a multitude of playful children surrounded me. The women giggled, and the men just stared. Karam told me I could take photos and sat me down in a plastic chair in an area where the men were grouped. I smiled at the expressionless fellows, who clearly did not know what to make of me and didn't speak a word of English. Ahmad stood to the side trying to suppress his laughter as he watched me attempt to communicate with them.

Dubious men at the family gathering

Karam took my hand and brought me over to meet the women. Followed by the gaggle of kids, he asked me to sit down on the ground. I didn't understand at first that he had just invited me to take part in the family's Holy Week feast! I couldn't believe it. All I wanted was to take a photo, and here I was, joining their family dinner.

Sitting on the ground with about two dozen women and children, I was presented with a large plate of lamb. Eating with our fingers, we dipped homemade flatbread into rice and sauce. I made my best attempt to return the culinary favor and offered my hosts some trail mix, which they'd never tasted but liked. (It must have been the M&Ms.) I was flattered and grateful for their generous hospitality, but it was time to go. *"Shukran; al-salamu alyakum,"* I said, *"Thank you very much; may peace be upon you."*

Hospitality of strangers

Ahmad kidded me in the days that followed, saying that they were probably still talking about me. I could not stop thinking how exceptional the experience was. Would an American family invite a stranger who knocked on their door asking to take their picture into the house for Thanksgiving dinner?

The next day, we continued our drive east toward Iraq. We were in the middle of the desert. There was nothing but sand. As luck would have it, it was here, in the middle of nowhere, where we got a flat tire.

Thankfully, a good Samaritan and his wife stopped to help us. But he no sooner got the spare on than the

Flat tire in the middle of the desert

air hissed out of it. There was no choice but to drive more than thirty miles on the tire's rim to the nearest town to get it fixed.

This good Samaritan offered to drive the car to the town and back to get help. Ahmad, the good Samaritan's wife, and I all had to stay behind because additional weight was not good when driving on the rim.

Our good Samaritan was gone for nearly four hours. Of course, there were moments when I thought we'd never see our car again and that we'd been left for dead. Ahmad continued to assure me not to worry. Hours went by as we waited under a relentless, piercing sun. Then, lo and behold, came our good Samaritan, smiling, the tire fixed. I, of course, insisted on paying him for his kindness, but he would have none of it.

Again, I pose the question: can you imagine such a scenario in America, where a guy and his wife would take the better part of their day to help a perfect stranger—and ask for nothing in return?

We circled south, down the Iraqi border to Palmyra, passing isolated Bedouin families. Located in eastern Syria, Palmyra is one of the most notable archaeological sites in the world, and the most important in Syria. Once home to fifty thousand people, it also was a significant caravan stop on the Silk Road.

The last part of my journey took me even further south to the Jordanian border, where we visited Bosra, with archives dating to 4000 BC. It's known for having the most well-preserved Greco-Roman amphitheater in existence. Buried under sand and totally obscured, the twenty-nine thousand-seat structure was only uncovered in the twentieth century.

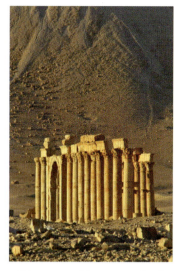

Palmyra, one of the greatest cultural centers of the ancient world

Palmyra's tetrapylon suffered intentional destruction by ISIS.

Finally, I went to the Shahba district where some of Syria's Druze live. An offshoot of Shiite Islam, their faith has survived mainly because of the secrecy that surrounds it. Not only is conversion to or from the faith prohibited, but only the elite Druze leaders have full access to the religious doctrine, which is contained in seven holy books that exist only in handwritten copies.

Syria was an amazing adventure. I had tried not to have any expectations going in, and quickly learned that history, religion, and politics are inseparable in defining Syria's culture. I enjoyed long talks with Ahmad about religions—and about the similarities among them. He was saddened by the West's negative impressions that Muslims should be feared.

The civil war in Syria began just after I left. As it continues, killing and displacing more families than one can comprehend, I think of these wonderful, generous people and their unforgettable acts of kindness. Worrying about them keeps me up at night. I last heard from my guide, Ahmad, about a year after the war was heating up. He had no work, and he and his family were trying to figure out

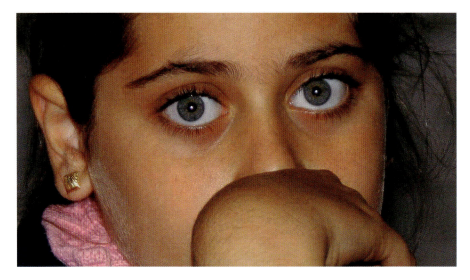

Pensive young student

how to get out of Syria. I have not heard from him since. Were they and the others I spent time with able to flee their homeland? Are they still alive?

With so much at stake in the Middle East, we can only hope for meaningful peace negotiations. *Inshallah!*

Tattooed women in Chin State

MYANMAR

Land of Contradictions

Rarely in my traveling life have I been so surprised and so amazed as I was in Myanmar. Formerly called Burma, Myanmar is home to an incredible 126 different ethnic groups that speak hundreds of languages and dialects. I was uneasy visiting this country, which has one of the most ruthless militaries in the world. Myanmar holds a terrible human rights record. Many groups have tried unsuccessfully to stop the violence and encourage fair elections, but its dictatorship held a tight grip on anyone who might assemble or speak out against the government, punishing peaceful protesters and their families.

This paranoid and isolationist regime served as a backdrop for my 2008 trip. I had to be careful. I dared not speak about the government to my guide, Zaw Zaw, until he completely trusted me. Otherwise, I might put him in danger. Journalists were not permitted to visit, and because I carried a large camera and lens, I was easily mistaken for press. All my emails to the United States and key websites were blocked.

Opening My Cultural Lens

Before my visa and letter of permission to enter the country were granted, my itinerary had to be approved by the government. My guide also had a large stack of copies of my passport, visa, and other documents that he had to present to everyone along the way, including hotels and checkpoints. Officials knew my every move.

Zaw Zaw was with me the entire time. I had local guides for access into villages, and I had translators for the many tribal languages, but Zaw Zaw and I were joined at the hip. Surveillance notwithstanding, he was so proud to show me his beautiful country.

Myanmar is a fiercely religious Buddhist country, where faith centers on kindness, modesty, and respect for elders, family, and community—a harsh contrast to the cruel ruling military command.

Nuns at a Buddhist meditation center

Lunchtime at the monastery

I began in Yangon, formerly called Rangoon. Visually, it's a city of contrasts. Its landscape is dotted with old, weathered buildings alongside golden pagodas. The first thing I noticed is the standard attire for most men and women. They both wear a longyi—a sarong-like skirt that's very comfortable and practical in the oppressive heat, and keeps them covered when visiting temples or monasteries.

Many women and children (and some men) also paint their faces with a paste called *thanakha*, a traditional makeup.

Zaw Zaw and I flew to west-central Myanmar, where we took a boat down the Irrawaddy River. Then we picked up a jeep to drive into the mountains that separate Myanmar from Bangladesh. On gnarly, potholed dirt roads, we drove ten long hours west into the mountains. We passed rice fields fed from the Irrawaddy River. Our destination was Mindat, a remote village that few outsiders, or Burmese, have ever been to.

Girl wearing thanakha makeup

Working in the fields, Irrawaddy Delta

In western Myanmar, people combine spiritual beliefs.

My accommodations were loosely wired for electricity, but it rarely worked. There was no running or hot water, just a washtub. It was chilly in the mountains and colder at night. All my meals were taken at a tiny local tea shop—breakfast, lunch, and dinner. No one spoke a word of English, but everyone was friendly and eager to take care of me.

My first full day there was tough. We trekked for hours on a steep, rocky, slippery path to get to the other side of the valley. We finally entered a village; home to the Mun Chin tribe. The Mun Chin, Tibeto-Burmese people who came here in 500 BC, used to be animists, but some became Christians following the arrival of the missionaries during the British colonial period.

Mun Chin women wearing traditional headdresses

Today, as with many tribal cultures, they combine Christianity with other spiritual beliefs.

I was greeted by the headman, who was also the shaman. Zaw Zaw told me that only a handful of foreigners have ever been to this isolated village and that I just might be the only American to visit this tribe since the missionaries before WWII! Because they have few visitors, the residents were excited to show me their rituals, performed by the shaman and the village leaders. (I kindly passed on the one where they sacrificed animals.)

Mun people are very serious about predictions and fortune-telling. The headman cut a small hole in both sides of an egg and blew out the yolk and white. He then scratched a line on the egg with a knife and pressed a hot bamboo stick fresh from the fire onto the shell. The heat made a line where he pressed. If the line is straight, your luck is good, he explained. Another man peeled ginger into small pieces. If the pieces drop to the ground face up, it's good news. These rituals guide decision-making.

Dancing and storytelling rituals   Mun Chin fortune-telling

I couldn't wait to witness my host's dance. The entire village came to watch. Some of the dances aim to bring the community close together to fend off the enemy; others ask for a good crop. The dancing began with storytelling, using movements partly based on martial arts to show how they fought off animals and enemies.

Back in Mindat, I spent time with several different tribal groups famous for their facial tattoos, a custom that began in the eleventh century when young girls essentially disfigured their faces to protect themselves from slavery or from capture by ruling princes. The practice decreased after the missionaries arrived, but there are still girls and women today with these tattoos.

Another tribal group in the area are the Dai, whose tattoos are a much darker color. The Dai women are also recognized for their long earrings, which stretch the ear lobe.

I met an eighty-five-year-old woman who was held in high esteem in her community because she was one of only two people left who

Opening My Cultural Lens

Makan woman, talented flutist   Mindat's ethnic minority is targeted by the military.

could play a flute with her nose. She was most respected for her skill. I tried it. The result was she retained her well-deserved title.

It was time to go back down the mountain. I was having breakfast at the tea shop while Zaw Zaw, who knew everyone, was helping out in the kitchen. I was eating my toast and peanut butter when a man at the table next to me said hello and started chatting in English. We made small talk, then he stood and quite nonchalantly said, "I should tell you that I'm with the Burmese FBI."

I just looked at him and said, "All righty, then. Well, have a nice day!" He got up, hopped on his motorbike, and left. When Zaw Zaw and I got back in the car, I told him what had happened. He said the man was probably sent to Mindat to make sure I didn't deviate from my schedule.

In the middle of our ten-hour drive back to Bagan, we stopped for lunch at a little outdoor restaurant. Afterward, Zaw Zaw asked me if I had noticed a couple of men sitting off in a corner of the restaurant. He said they were both police, and again, were checking on me. Zaw Zaw had known about this all along but chose not to tell me as he thought it would upset me. I told him I'd been through worse—and at that point, I hadn't yet been to North Korea.

Bagan is the heart of Myanmar's Buddhist culture. It is home to thousands of temples, with new ones being built all the time. They don't just dot the landscape—they cover it. Back in the eleventh century, the king began an extensive building program that Marco Polo called one of the greatest sights in the world. We climbed to the top of a thousand-year-old stupa to watch the soft pastel sunset over Bagan. The majestic view of the green countryside overlooks thousands of ancient pagodas, each one with a Buddha inside. I couldn't take enough photos from this vantage.

Bagan's landscape boasts thousands of temples

Golden Shwezigon Pagoda

From Bagan, we flew east to Heho, the front door to the Inle Lake region—the Venice of Burma. People here live in countless little water villages with houses and monasteries built on stilts. The self-sufficient communities are rich agricultural centers that grow flowers, vegetables, and fruit on floating islands.

Most of the people here are of the Intha tribe, best known for their unusual fishing and boating skills. An Intha from Inle, Zaw Zaw used to be a fisherman here and couldn't wait to demonstrate the one-legged technique, which allows them to paddle and fish at the same time. The fishermen navigate their boats by standing at the stern on one leg and wrapping their other leg around an oar. They push forward with their arm, and back with their leg. This technique enables anglers to spot fish while standing up in the boat. They'll first look for bubbles from the fish, then take a long pole and slap the surface to get the fish moving. Then they drop a large cone-shaped basket in the water to trap the fish and release a net to catch them. Zaw Zaw masterfully displayed his skill at all of this. He asked me if I'd like to try. "Oh darn," I said, "I didn't bring a swimsuit."

Zaw Zaw demonstrating the one-legged fisherman technique, Inle Lake

Our entire time at Inle was spent on the water, moving from village to village by canoe, and visiting the countless monasteries that house many young monks. Beginning at age seven, Buddhist boys have a religious duty to become novice monks. Just as Buddha left his own family to seek enlightenment, the monks live in a monastery. When they enter the monastery, they are given only a handful of possessions, including a robe, belt, footwear, razor, umbrella, glass, and an alms bowl. Boys can stay through high school, Zaw Zaw said, but then must decide if they want to commit their lives to becoming monks.

Long-necked woman, Padaung

I also met members of the Padaung tribe, known for the long-necked women who wear brass rings stacked high from their shoulders to their chins. Legend has it that women wore the rings to make them less attractive to enemy tribes that might have wanted to kidnap them. Today, in complete contrast, some believe the rings lengthen their necks, making the women more beautiful.

I am particularly fond of Buddhist countries, and Myanmar did not disappoint. The people shared the same compassionate dispositions as citizens of Bhutan, Tibet, and Mongolia, making Myanmar seem familiar, but also making it hard to reconcile that leaders of this extraordinarily kind country could commit such serious human rights violations.

Since I visited in 2008, the atrocities have continued. The government continues to persecute ethnic minority Rohingya Muslims and has terrorized other ethnic groups, including the Karen people. In 2021, the military ousted political leaders in a coup and arrested the popular pro-democracy Nobel Peace Prize winner, Aung San Suu Kyi.

Over the course of this long trip, I had forged a strong friendship with Zaw Zaw. When it was time to say goodbye, he brought his wife to the airport so she could meet the silly lady from America that had become so taken with his beautiful country. It's hard for me to leave many of my guides, knowing full well I may never see them again. Zaw Zaw taught me so much about Myanmar's culture and everyday life.

Myanmar's conflict impacts education.

Today, as I read the frightening headlines, I worry every day about Zaw Zaw and his family. How have they been affected, and what's in store for them next?

Myanmar's people are resilient. Through their challenges, they continue to practice the principles of their faith—compassion, kindness, and respect. These incredible people helped me understand that at a time when my country is wounded and facing our own difficulties, maybe we, too, can transcend the flaws of our nature, and together solve some of our most demanding problems because nothing is impossible.

Novice monks

MALI

Too Close to Danger

I'd hear it from folks all the time. "Geez, you've been everywhere except Timbuktu," they'd laugh, thinking I'd not heard that before. I'd always laugh along and reply, "Not yet."

It was about time.

There was a lot I wanted to see in Mali, which sits on the southern edge of the Sahara in northwestern Africa. One of the poorest coun-

Mali is threatened by corruption and political instability.

Kids caring for kids

tries on the planet, its desert conditions make even subsistence agriculture difficult. A majority of Malians live on only $2 per day. Life expectancy is only forty-nine years old, and 20 percent of Malian children die before the age of five. Daily life is a struggle.

I began my trip in Bamako, the capital, but was anxious to get out into the countryside to see some of Mali's ancient cultural sites. My guide, Moussa, and I hit the rugged road for an eight-hour drive to Djenné, famous for its distinctive adobe buildings made from mud bricks. Founded in the fourth century, Djenné has hardly changed since the middle ages when it was a center in the trans-Saharan gold trade.

Early the next morning, we visited one of the country's most notable sites, the Mosque of Djenné. When we arrived, I was told why we had to be there at the crack of dawn. Non-Muslims are not permitted to enter, but my guide knew the imam's son, who wanted to show me this beautiful mosque under the radar. It's who you know.

Mosque of Djenné

At the end of every rainy season, up to four thousand volunteers help replaster the mud walls that wash away. Wooden spars that jut out from the walls form part of the mosque's structure and serve as ladders when its fragile exterior needs repair. This main mosque is so crowded for Friday prayers that Muslims must pray in the hallways.

Outside of Djenné, we went to a village of about sixty people, all of whom were one extended family. While I was there, I was able to witness a naming ceremony. This is a Muslim tradition wherein the village men line up to approve the name of the neighborhood's new infant. Though I was not allowed to photograph the ritual, the town folk, including the mom (who did not have a voice in selecting a name), were happy to bring me into the fold to watch the festivities.

Sadly, garbage and litter were strewn everywhere. Their sanitary conditions were worse yet, and the dust—I was constantly covering my gear to protect it from fine particles that are not friendly to a camera.

We continued north to the huge Bandiagara Escarpment, one of the most impressive archaeological sites in West Africa. In the eleventh century, the Dogon built their houses on top of the inhospitable escarpment to protect themselves from the advancing Arabs. The vast region and UNESCO site has 289 architecturally fascinating mudbrick villages, many built into the sides of the steep cliffs. The villages uniquely feature clusters of rectangle thatched storage granaries. Women keep a separate granary for their own personal belongings, while the men keep seeds and grasses dry in theirs.

Pride amidst hardship

Dogon are Muslims and animists. Because the French introduced Christianity, villages have both churches and mosques—an interesting and religiously tolerant combination. The Dogon worship their ancestors and nomadic spirits, many ceremonies are performed in caves. Dogon funerals can be quite lively with singing, chanting, and drums—all helping get

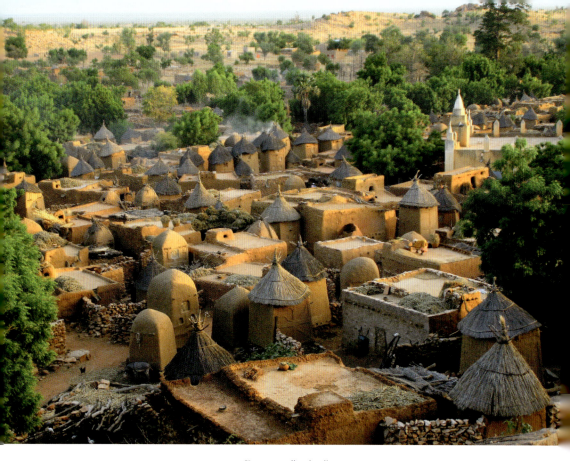

Dogon mudbrick village

rid of any evil spirits and helping the deceased person's soul enter the afterlife.

We had to get to our next village by foot. Very early the following day, in the still-cool morning, we began a two-hour hike down rugged, jagged cliffs. Once the sun rose, it was unrelenting, the light a piercing white. As we hiked, we passed through a small village when I noticed a sign that said "The Carter Center." It turned out Jimmy and Rosalynn Carter's charitable organization's global health program had boots on the ground here.

I was so excited. For years I've personally been involved with The Carter Center, which, in addition to its successful global peace initiatives, is deeply committed to improving health. The center had been teaching Malians how to combat devastating diseases. It's been working to eliminate the vicious Guinea worm disease and to control trachoma, and in this village, the center had just built a well and installed a water filtering system.

Curious villagers, Bandiagara Escarpment

Mali's child deprivation is 50 percent.

A few months after my Mali trip, I told President Carter what a thrill it was to just happen upon this remote village and see the center's work firsthand. He wasn't surprised, as, for many years, he's known all about my global adventures. With a big smile, he reminded me that there's a lot of work to do. His extraordinary involvement with and oversight of improving health in Mali is legendary. He said he hoped I did my part to emphasize the importance of clean water to those I met. Of course, Mr. President.

My main reason for coming to Mali was to reach the remote UNESCO World Heritage site, Timbuktu. There are a lot of poems and limericks that describe Timbuktu. It is said to be so far away that it resides "at the end of the world." Some of my friends actually thought it was a fictional place "on the road to nowhere." It was about time I put that myth to rest. Timbuktu is indeed a real place with a fascinating history.

Timbuktu was once a major commercial hub because it was located on the great trans-Saharan caravan route. Huge convoys of camels would spend weeks crossing the desert to get there. Significant mosques and universities were built as the city grew to become a center of Islamic learning and culture. However, in the sixteenth century, armies from Morocco invaded, killing Timbuktu's scholars and leaders and forcing others to flee. Its golden age came to an end, and the city has diminished ever since.

Harsh Sahara Desert

Djinguereber Mosque

Today, the population continues to decline in part due to regional fighting. When I was there in 2011, thirty-thousand people lived in this dusty town.

I wondered how Timbuktu got its name. Depending on which ethnic group tells the story, there are several variations. I happen to like this one: once upon a time, there was a woman named Bouchtou, which means large navel. She was put in charge of the settlement by the nomadic Tuareg herdsmen while they were away. *Tom* means "water well," so the name *Tombuchtu* means "the well of the mother with the large navel." You can't make this stuff up.

The Sahara is a harsh place. The only ethnic group that has been capable of surviving such difficult conditions is the nomadic Tuareg, predominantly Muslim Berbers who live in several northern African countries. There are nearly a million in Mali. For years, many northern Tuaregs have felt marginalized by Mali's government and have called for full representation by forming the National Movement for the Liberation of Azawad (NMLA). This group seeks to establish an autonomous Azawad region in Mali.

Col. Muammar Gaddafi, former prime minister of Libya, was impressed with the tenacity of the Tuaregs. He brought them into his army and rewarded their loyalty. The rebel Tuaregs gave Gaddafi protection as he hid in the Sahara during the Libyan revolution. Since Gaddafi's death in 2011, his son has been welcomed by the NMLA, which continues to revolt against Mali's government.

Colorfully dressed in Timbuktu's dusty streets

When I visited Timbuktu, I did not see any other Westerners. That's not to say Westerners weren't there; I just never saw any. As a result, I—a light-skinned, light-haired foreigner—stuck out like a sore thumb as I walked the streets and visited mosques and outdoor markets. One afternoon, while strolling and photographing, I met Mohamed, a young Tuareg who had just arrived in Timbuktu after a grueling, ten-day trek across the Sahara. He had to travel at night because it was too hot for both the nomads and their camels during the day. Mohamed came to buy goods and souvenirs he planned to resell back home. Of course, I asked if I could take his picture.

He was decked out in a beautiful bright indigo robe and turban. Called the "Blue People of the Sahara," the Tuareg wear layers of loose-fitting cotton, which ingeniously slows the evaporation of sweat. Their turban and veil, called a *tagelmust*, can be ten yards long. In addition to pro-

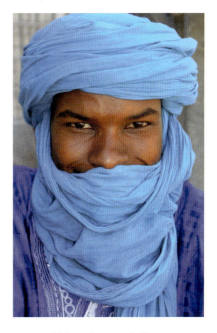

Mohamed, a nomadic Tuareg

viding protection from the harsh desert sands, men wear the veil as a rite of passage into manhood and to ward off evil spirits.

We started to chat. Mohamed was practicing his English and wanted to learn more about America and particularly tourism, as he had his hopes set on opening a shop back in his hometown. In Timbuktu, some are wary of the Tuareg because of their rebellious nature. As a single woman traveling alone, people all over the world are just as curious about me as I am about them. I was protected by Mohamed, and my afternoon felt welcoming and safe.

Wandering Timbuktu's streets

But the day after I left Timbuktu, I learned about a chilling incident, one I had, thank God, just missed. An armed militant group stormed a restaurant in the city center, murdered a Western tourist, and kidnapped three others. The attack was linked to a radical al-Qaeda cell that demanded ransoms and prisoners released, a common terrorist tactic. All foreigners were immediately air-lifted out of the entire country. Thankfully, I had already left, just hours before.

The murder and kidnappings were particularly disturbing because while I was in Timbuktu, I recalled not seeing another Westerner. I also thought about the hours I spent wandering about the town alone, not with Mohamad. I was quite the sitting duck. People ask me all the time if I have ever been afraid while traveling. I honestly never had, though I now admit the Timbuktu experience made me reflect how close I may have come to danger.

Sadly, because of the same regional fighting that's decimating its population, Timbuktu has since earned another designation. The ancient city was placed on the UNESCO List of World Heritage in Danger.

NORTH KOREA

One-Sided Mirror

Globe trekkers, like me, often seek out destinations that are off the beaten path. No place on earth meets that measure more than mysterious North Korea. In 2010, I learned that North Korea was offering rare visas to select Americans. I applied, jumping at the extraordinary chance to visit one of the most perplexing and isolated spots on the planet. To have a peek at this seemingly forbidden land would be a once-in-a-lifetime experience.

My local agent had never worked with any US firm that had done business in North Korea, so I had to arrange this trip on my own. I was able to find an agency located in China that represented North Korea. Getting my documents approved took months.

Since 1945, the state-controlled ruling Democratic People's Republic of Korea (called the DPRK) has been run by three family members—supreme leaders. This regime distrusts outsiders and is fearful of external political and economic leverage. It's also not wild about spies. Therefore, North Korea is suspicious of American visitors. I needed to demonstrate that just because I ran a photography-based cultural nonprofit, I was not a journalist or a spy. To make sure I wasn't on a media assignment, I provided the agency with information about my nonprofit and photography and my intent to visit. I also did my homework about what was permitted and what was not.

To obtain the visa, I needed to go to China. My meeting with the agency was scheduled for the very morning my flight was to depart Beijing for Pyongyang. I flew into Beijing two days before a briefing so I would be rested and prepared, luggage in hand, and able to get to the airport on time. The best-laid plans. I took a taxi to the agency and walked in the door at 9:00 a.m. sharp, just as the office opened. I was greeted by the manager and asked to watch some videos about North Korea. He gave me materials to read, some of which described what my itinerary would entail as well as further explanations of what was permitted and what was not. The rules were *uber*-strict, and I knew full well what I could not do. After all, I did not want to end up being a headline on CNN.

My flight was supposed to leave at 1:25 p.m. I continued to read and watch the videos, but time was flying by, and I was getting nervous. The clock was nearing 11:00 a.m. I just flew 6,300 miles and could not miss this flight. I was a long way from the airport; I had no idea what the process was going to be like at the

Patriotic billboards seen everywhere

ticket counter—I'd have to get through customs, and there'd be my final processing at the gate. I was officially panicking.

The manager finally handed over my documents, including an approved visa. I took a deep breath and thanked him as I took off running through the office, grabbed some young agent by the arm, and begged him to get me a taxi! The cab raced through the busy Beijing traffic to the airport.

I found the nearly empty ticket counter for Air China, checked in, and sprinted toward the assigned gate. Except I could not see any visible signage. It was 1:05 p.m. I ran down one concourse then another, confused and begging for help. No one seemed to know, and I didn't have time to go back to the ticket counter. I then accosted some employee in an electric cart, who said, "Not sure, but try that way." I took his advice and dashed down some stairs toward the right gate, where a woman was about to close the door to a bus that would carry passengers to the airplane parked on the tarmac. Still running, my heart was pounding, and I was soaked with sweat. I waved frantically, praying she'd see me before she closed the door. She looked up and caught my wild eyes just in time.

The Pyongyang airport was quite ordinary, although at passport control I had to surrender my cell phone, which I got back when I departed. My three—yes, three—guides stood to welcome me—one driver, one riding shotgun, and the third in back with me. They all were very friendly and gracious.

My hotel was a large, high-quality property that primarily catered to Chinese travelers. I've been to plenty of countries where I've been surveilled, so I always wondered if North Korea would provide the same amenity. My experience has been that state-run countries, if you don't disobey, are all the safer for visitors because these places don't tolerate anyone breaking the rules, especially their own citizens.

Opening My Cultural Lens

View of Pyongyang

Crowded streetcar, Pyongyang

For the next five days, I would be taken to the area's important sites, statues, and monuments, all promoting North Korea's *Juche* political system and its views of history—particularly with respect to the United States. Every person, billboard, book, and song—everything, all the time—promotes the nation's ideas of dominance, efficiency, and wisdom. Juche means that nothing has value beyond its use, and its doctrines address material possessions and self-sacrifice. People are required to learn, accept, and turn their hearts over to Juche. Their fervor comes from the Great Leader, who is the supreme representative of their interests. Their identities are tied to the great leaders, who are worshiped. Their ideology permeates every part of life.

Political Juche signage

Patriotic reading in a DPRK bookstore

My restricted itinerary was approved by the government, and I was always accompanied by my guides. As a visitor, if I was not comfortable with these limitations, I would be best advised not to travel there. So why did I want to go? Because there is no other place like it.

It rained for most of my stay, which hampered my photography. But we pressed on, visiting sites dedicated to the Kims: Kim Il Sung, the Great Leader; and Kim Jong Il, the Dear Leader. I was there just before Kim Jung-Un, the next son in line, took power.

DPRK soldier

Mansu Hill Grand Monument

My guides first took me to the memorial palace, called the Kumsusan Palace of the Sun, which serves as the mausoleum of Kim Il Sung. This all-but-holy site set the stage for my experience in North

Korea. I was required to dress up. Photography was not permitted. After the security check, I silently and solemnly entered and followed an elaborate procession on a moving walkway down long hallways. The rigorous entry procedure involved passing through a "clean room" where air was blasted to remove any dust from my clothes and shoes. I could not hold anything in my hands, and when standing, I could not place my hands behind my back, only at my sides or in front. I entered with a few other (North Koreans) in rows of four. When I got to the body of the Great Leader, where I was required to bow at three sides of his body, I circled clockwise. Then I walked in line out of the room.

Rainy day at Kumsusan Palace of the Sun

As the days went by, I visited numerous key sites, including: the Juche Tower; the Arch of Reunification, representing a proposed reunification with South Korea; the Arch of Triumph, commemorating North Korea's resistance to Japan; and the USS Pueblo, which the North Koreans claimed entered their waters in 1968.

Several hours were needed to see the huge Victorious Fatherland Liberation War Museum depicting, from North Korea's point of view, its victory in the Korean War. I was escorted by a uniformed guide who described each exhibit in-depth. The tour included a panoramic display and motion picture describing the Battle of Taejon, where US forces were pushed back in an attempt to defend the headquarters of the Twenty-Fourth Infantry Division.

Murals of the Great Leader

I visited the Mangyongdae Children's Palace, which offers classes in music, circus, and dance for gifted youth. The palace has 120 rooms, a swimming pool, gymnasium, library, and a two thousand-seat theater. One of the most memorable sites was the opulent Pyongyang Metro. I was only allowed to ride—accompanied, of course—between select stops. During peak rush hour, reportedly up to seven hundred thousand passengers ride its system of sixteen stations. The subway is located one hundred meters underground with marble walls, chandeliers, mosaics, bronze work, and huge hand-painted murals. Its magnificence reminded me of the grand design of the Moscow Metro in Russia.

But nothing I'd ever seen prepared me for the Mass Games, when talented young people perform for several days at the state-of-the-art, 150,000-seat, outdoor Rungrado May Day Stadium. It's called the Greatest Show on Earth, and rightly so. The larger-than-life extravaganza features more than a hundred thousand students, some only five years old, who perform in perfectly synchronized gymnastics, acrobatics, song, dance, and martial arts. As impressive is the backdrop on the far seats of the stadium where twenty thousand children flawlessly change colored flashcards every fifteen to thirty seconds to create different scenes. There were landscapes, images, photos, and artistic arrangements all executed to perfection, even on this night, in the rain.

Mangyongdae Children's Palace

Opening My Cultural Lens

Mass Games features 20,000 children changing flash cards

Choreographed dancers praise the Great Leader, Mass Games

The significance of the two-hour show is to illustrate patriotic Juche themes while displaying discipline and efficiency, for they say, the slightest mistake would ruin the entire show. (I'd hate to be the one that screws up.) It's an enormous responsibility, and there's a sense of great pride for those selected to train and perform. The night that the Dear Leader attends, I'm told, is like performing before God.

For many reasons, I intentionally did not ask my guides too many questions. I didn't want to enter into any conversations that would put any of them—or me—at risk. I never spoke to anyone without my guide's permission, and I asked them in advance each and every time I wanted to take a photograph. Even after they assured me I could take a photo of this monument or that memorial, I asked twice, just to be sure they knew I was not going to sneak a photo and cause them—or me—any trouble.

After spending several days in Pyongyang, we finally got out of town to visit the DMZ, the most heavily militarized border in the world. President Bill Clinton once called it the "scariest place on Earth." Now, in North Korea, I was about to visit the same demilitarized zone that I previously visited from the South Korea side and walk into the same blue building that houses the infamous Military Armistice Commission conference room. The room looked all too familiar. One side of the neutral zone room is in South Korea, and the other is in North Korea. Visitors ceremoniously walk around a table to enter both countries.

The DMZ is about 160 miles from Pyongyang, so I was able to see some of the countryside, which is mainly agricultural with some manufacturing. I was not allowed to travel anywhere else, outside my hotel or outside their watchful eyes.

DMZ building from the North

The Great Leader, signage in the countryside

Another watchful eye

A cautious father

I was treated exceptionally well, though. I had great accommodations, wonderful food, and guides who did their duty to show me the best of their country. I behaved myself and made certain every photo I took had their blessing. I was later assured I could post my photos and talk about my experience, one that allowed me to see and learn just a little about this mysterious place.

For years, America has had a tense and ominous relationship with North Korea. What will become of the association between these two countries? What does the rest of North Korea look like—its daily life, citizens' access to information, and the wellbeing of its people?

What about its children? What will their lives look like?

And, will we all see peace?

Sheikh Lotfallah Mosque, Esfahan

IRAN

Another Cultural Faux Pas

Unfortunately, when we think of Iran, most of us know only what we hear in the news. Worse yet, too many believe Iranians are all radical extremists, and all Muslims are terrorists. These impressions are so unfair and could not be further from the truth. I visited Iran in 2016 after diplomatic agreements created a path for the United States to lift its sanctions on certain oil and finance sectors, as well as global trading and Iranian exports, such as carpets made by some of the world's finest artisans. I found the Iranians I met to be welcoming, curious, and ecstatic to have a fresh chance to get back on their feet.

As our flight was pulling up to the gate in Tehran, I noticed the women on board were quickly getting out their headscarves. Wom-

Girls checking their messages

en must always wear a hijab, no exceptions. I was struggling to keep my hijab in place, but a lovely, elderly Iranian woman could tell I was new at this—she smiled sweetly and gave me a hand. I stepped off the airplane with everyone else walking down the jetway, but I was pulled over by an authority who escorted me into a private room. *Already?* I thought, *I haven't been here for two seconds and I'm in trouble?*

The room had a few uniformed agents and one other non-Iranian passenger, whom I sat next to as we waited for instructions. I was ushered over to a desk where I presented my passport, visa, and documents. I was asked about the purpose of my visit, what I intended to do in Iran and why, where I was staying, who I was seeing, and what Iranian agency I was working with. Months earlier, to get my visa, I provided information to the Iranian Embassy that addressed the same questions I was now being asked by the agent.

The entire process took nearly an hour. In the meantime, they had fetched my checked baggage, inspected it, and had it waiting for me as I left the screening room. I thought I was good to go, but then they next asked me to sit in a waiting room (which I think they wanted me to believe was a lounge) until I was met by my guide. I sat there wondering how he'd find me because I hadn't gone through general customs, was not in the baggage claim area, and certainly was not in the general terminal. After about fifteen minutes, a nice young man introduced himself.

"You must be Gail," said Mahmoud, my guide. I had arrived in Iran. That wasn't so bad.

Like other Middle Eastern nations, Iran is complex. Because of its juxtaposition in the greater Middle East, Iran is in the center of the most fluid geopolitical region in the world. To know Iran today, I needed to understand some of its history, which is entwined with its religion and its politics.

For hundreds of years, empires and dynasties came and went. Around 330 BC, Alexander the Great defeated the Persian armies, torched Persepolis, and destroyed the first Persian empire. Then, when Chinggis Khan and his merry band of grandsons arrived in the thirteen century, they conquered and destroyed many Persian cities and the country's documented history.

Iran's religion is unquestionably central to understanding this culture. Iran is a Shiite country in a Muslim world that is mostly Sunni. After Muhammad died, Islam was divided over who should succeed him. Because Muhammad had no heir (and therefore, no successor), two sects resulted—the Sunnis and the Shia. Until this time, Iran had Shiite followers, but Sunni Islam began to spread to Iran from Syria. This divided some of the population. After Muhammad died, leadership was passed down to twelve successors. Hussein was one of them.

Cleric in Tehran

In early Islam, the Shia supported Ali, who was the son-in-law of Muhammad. When Ali was murdered, his chief opponent became caliph, the chief Muslim ruler. But Ali's son, Hussein, refused to accept him, and fights between the two erupted. When Hussein and his followers were massacred in the battle at Karbala, the Shia cult of martyrdom began, and so did their struggle against injustice and oppression. Again, the Shia are a minority, with 85 percent of today's Muslims being Sunni.

Fast forward to the twentieth century and, eventually, to present-day Iran.

In 1921, soldier Reza Khan staged a coup, took control of the army, and became the Shah. He wanted to completely modernize Iran the same way other regional leaders were doing in their countries. He also wanted women to wear western dress, and made it illegal to wear the chador, the full black cloth wrapped around the head and body. These measures proved to be difficult because many traditional women didn't embrace this change, which is still true today.

For thousands of years, Iran was called Persia, but in 1934, Reza Khan changed the name to Iran, which means "of noble origin." During WWII, while Khan said he wanted Iran to be a neutral country, he instead sympathized with the Nazis, so it was no surprise that the British, Soviets, and Americans ousted him. His son, Mohammad Reza Pahlavi, became the shah.

Slowly changing, Iranian law still favors men.

This new shah was originally backed by the United States, which wanted him to continue to advance women's rights, land reform, and get rid of the power of the clerics. In 1962, Ayatollah Khomeini was emerging as an opposition leader to the shah. An ayatollah is the highest rank of a Shiite cleric. By 1974, Iran's oil sales and its economy plummeted, and everyone blamed the shah. By 1978, demonstrations resulted, and the shah responded with violence. Soon the shah fled, and Ayatollah Khomeini became supreme leader and set out to make Iran a clergy-dominated Islamic republic. He succeeded through brutality.

In 1979, as America's support decreased, a group of Iranian university students took over the US Embassy and held fifty-two Americans hostage, and 444 days later, after a failed rescue attempt, they were finally released.

In the 1980s, Iraq's Saddam Hussein began an eight-year war with Iran over a piece of oil-rich Iranian land. One million Iranians died, and millions more had no work. Today, streets are lined with photos of those martyrs who lost their lives fighting that war with Iraq. Khomeini died in 1989, and Ali Khamenei succeeded him as ayatollah. But Iran was in shambles.

Then, in 1997, Mohammad Khatami—a liberal—was elected and tried to reform Iran, but the conservatives slammed that door.

Photos of martyrs line many streets.

The guardian council vetoed everything, barred liberals from running for office, and killed or imprisoned any opposition. For the next twenty years, nuclear issues increased along with global sanctions against Iran. But in 2016, when I was there, the sanctions had been momentarily lifted, and Iranians were hopeful for economic improvements, which had already begun.

Yes, this is a lot to digest, but understanding this recent history was necessary as I set out to travel in this complex land.

Mahmoud helped me navigate Iran's strict rules, especially those placed on women. To begin my adventure, we flew to the southern Iran city of Shiraz. Shiraz is the provincial capital of Fars and the birthplace of its Persian language, Farsi. Shiraz is known for poetry and has been the birthplace and resting place for some of the great Persian poets.

I first realized Mahmoud's sense of humor when we were sitting in the Tehran gate area waiting for our flight. He told me Shiraz is called the "nose job capital of the world." He said a lot of Iranian women (who are already strikingly gorgeous) go to Shiraz to get a nose job to enhance their beauty. As we watched passengers stroll by, Mahmoud would say, "Ten o'clock," slyly suggesting I look to see a probable candidate. He was a funny man.

Architecture students

Relaxing in a café

Iran is blessed with numerous World Heritage sites featuring stunning architecture, and many of them are found in Shiraz. The Shah Cheragh shrine is one of the Shiites' holiest sites in all of Iran. The mausoleum houses the shrines of the two brothers of Imam Reza, both descendants of the Prophet Muhammad. One of the brothers was executed. I was told about the Shia legend that said after they cut off his head, he took a few steps and put his head back on before he died. It makes sense to me. Non-Muslims had previously not been permitted inside that shrine, but they eased that rule by the time I was allowed in. I needed to wear a full chador and could only get in through a dedicated women's entrance.

Iran

Nasir al-Mulk, the Pink Mosque

Photographing some of these colorful mosques was a joy. The Nasir al-Mulk Mosque, also known as the "Pink Mosque," is a kaleidoscope of stained glass. Thousands of painted tiles and arched, carved pillars shine over brilliant Persian rugs. These architects completely understood the significance of light, using the sun to reflect the vivid colors. The Vakil Mosque features a vaulted prayer hall with elegantly carved columns and exquisite tile work. The mihrab— a semicircular niche in the wall—is located in the back of the mosque.

Mihrab of Jameh Mosque

Muslims pray facing the mihrab, which is in the direction of Mecca.

We drove north to another UNESCO landmark, the famous archaeological site of Persepolis, a phenomenal example of this ancient empire when about five thousand people lived here. Persepolis became the ceremonial capital and a symbol for the entire empire. But in 321 BC, along came Alexander the Great, who sacked and burned Persepolis after an epic drinking bout (though he was sober enough to remove its extensive library beforehand). Thankfully, in the 1930s, the ruins of the capital of the Persian Kingdom were excavated, uncovering a grand city with a palace, treasury, and sculptures depicting life at the time.

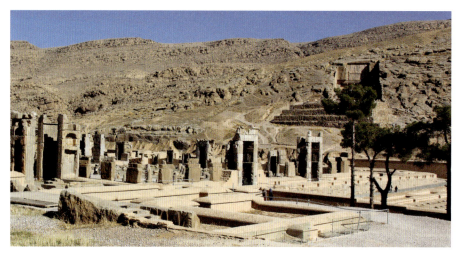

The ancient site of Persepolis

The entire eastern plateau of this huge country is covered by two deserts, which we drove through in central Iran to get to Yazd, a center of Islamic learning, also famous for its sizable community of Zoroastrians. Zoroastrianism used to be the primary religion in the Persian Empire. It was one of the first monotheistic religions, which scholars believe influenced Judaism, Christianity, and Islam. We visited a fire temple, which contains a sacred fire that has burned since

470 AD—that's more than 1,550 years! The fire represents the light of God and is never extinguished.

The centerpiece of Yazd is the stunning twelfth-century Jami Mosque—the city's big Friday congregational mosque and the oldest Friday mosque in Iran. It's the first Islamic building to incorporate the four-courtyard design used today in Islamic mosque architecture.

During my visit to this Shiite country, I saw black flags everywhere—on storefronts, roadsides, offices, and homes—recognizing Ashura, a national holiday when the Shia annually mourn the unjust killing of Hussein, the Prophet's grandson. It's one of the most tragic incidents in Islam. Mahmoud and I watched one of many dramatic outdoor reenactments, which helped me understand the degree to which the Shia mourn his martyrdom.

One of my favorite spots in Iran is Esfahān, which is the center of the greatest concentration of Islamic monuments in the country. We started out at the Chehel Sotoun Palace, a grand pavilion built for entertainment purposes by Shah Abbas II in the mid-1600s. He had a lot of parties. The elaborate palace contains many cypress columns, frescoes, and paintings and reflects the skill of the artisans and architects of the day. We also spent time at the historic Imam Square, the second-largest plaza in the world, with a huge fountain that fills the center of the complex.

Rays of sunshine filter through the amazing Sheikh Lotfallah Mosque, which is one of Esfahān's most historical monuments. It was built by Shah Abbas as a family mosque for his father-in-law. The complex also includes a large palace with a unique wooden ceiling. I climbed up to the top to have a look at the palace's incredible music room. The vaulted mudbrick ceilings are carved and painted, and its deep, circular niches are perfect for acoustics.

I was surprised to learn that not everyone in Iran is devout, and many Muslims do not attend Friday prayers. In Esfahān, on Fridays, instead of going to the mosque, I found thousands of lo-

Opening My Cultural Lens

cals gathered alongside a river, spending the day with their families and friends. They lay out a carpet, take off their shoes, and enjoy a picnic. I was invited by several families to sit and join them for tea. Little kids followed me everywhere.

Friday picnics, Esfahān

Under some of the bridges' archways, I heard young men lined up, singing love songs. This is an interesting tradition in Esfahān. I don't know if all these guys were single, attached, recently broken up, or what, but they are romantics! Here they were, under the bridges, showing off their talented solo voices. They took turns, one at a time, singing various verses of popular Persian love songs.

Friendly family

I honestly did not know what to expect in Iran. Not only did I learn more about its deep history and ancient sites, I also found Iranian people to be extremely kind to me, especially as an American. They were curious, friendly, and welcoming. They made me feel safe, even though Iranian women lack freedom. Women here can vote, drive, and buy property, and they're very well educated. In fact, two-thirds of the university students are women, although they are restricted from studying certain subjects and from getting the best jobs. They remain second-class citizens to men. Iranian women want an end to discrimination societally, culturally, and legally—not just policy change; women want rights.

Since my visit in 2016, relations between the United States and Iran have crumbled. Distrust has returned. Peaceful initiatives have diminished, and punishing sanctions were restored. Tensions are palpable. I am well aware of today's se-

Students eager for dialogue

vere political differences and pray meaningful discussions and peaceful negotiations can someday resume. I remember what I experienced when I was there. I saw a country desperate to get back on its feet economically, and I enjoyed a visit with people who were moving forward with their lives and who, in the process, embraced me as an American.

Having spent three weeks together, Mahmoud and I had become good friends. We enjoyed enlightening discussions and traded stories about Iran and America that gave us both a better understanding of our cultures. He had an easygoing personality with a wicked sense of humor, which I adored. We teased each other mercilessly, and I loved every minute.

On my last day in Iran, the time had come to bid farewell. We were in Tehran in a hotel lobby filled with people—all men, as I recall. Mahmoud and I didn't know what to do or how to say goodbye. After all, in this country, a woman is not even permitted to shake hands with a man in public. As we both tried to figure out what to say and do next, Mahmoud just looked at me and said, "Oh, the heck with it," and gave me a big bear hug, which, needless to say, is frowned upon in this culture. It stopped every conversation from the guys in the lobby! I teared up, and Mahmoud, smiling and wet-eyed, dashed out the door.

Maasai village

TANZANIA

My Last Safari—Coming Full Circle

My cultural escapades first took root more than forty years ago, during my first African safari. I could have never known—never dreamed—where they'd take me. Or, more importantly, how they'd change me. So, it's fitting that as we bring this story to a close, we revisit Africa for my last safari, this time to Tanzania, right next door to my first adventure four decades earlier in Kenya.

The Kenya-Tanzania border has been problematic over the years. When I was last there, Kenya was struggling with terrorism at the hands of al-Shabaab, the radical Somali Islamist group. As a result, Tanzania was enjoying a boost in tourism at Kenya's expense. My main reason to visit Tanzania, however, was to learn more about the Maasai, and of course, to go on safari.

In Kilimanjaro, I met up with my guide, Joseph. We headed to Ngorongoro, the heart of Maasai land. On the way, we drove through Lake Manyara National Park, which sits on the edge of the Great Rift

Valley. Called the "Cradle of Mankind," it's a huge, three-thousand-mile-long fault that begins near the Red Sea and stretches through East Africa all the way down to Mozambique, creating an active volcanic range. It's a geological wonder.

Lions are among the African "Big 5" found in Ngorongoro.

Little oxpeckers feed off insects on the mighty rhino.

We arrived at our first Maasai village and were met by the number two guy, a friendly fellow in his early thirties who spoke English well. The sixty residents were members of his extended family. The Maasai continue to live much the way their ancestors did centuries ago. They're not concerned about the passing of time. Instead, their pastoral lives are governed by the rising and setting of the sun and the changing seasons.

Young Number Two, who liked being called by his Western name, James, invited me into his home. Made from mud, cow dung, grass sticks, and cow's urine, the simple oval-shaped dwelling contained separate areas for cooking and sleeping, and a place to protect the goats from any wild animals. Maasai men can have many wives. James told me the chief of this village has twelve wives, and while he wanted to meet me, he was just too tired. I'm sure he was. A dozen wives will do it.

James was not married yet, which was very unusual, but he explained it's a big responsibility to have a family, and in this culture, it's sure to be a large family. He had a playful sense of humor—my invitation to joke around. I told the bachelor he was a handsome devil and that he'd make a great catch. "Perhaps we should get married." He howled and thought it was the perfect idea. He couldn't wait to break the news to others, though I got some dubious looks from some of the women (especially the unmarried ones) in the village who heard about our plan. I don't think they found me particularly funny. My guide did, though. And so did James, who was still giggling as we drove away.

James, the village's most eligible bachelor

The Maasai's traditional beliefs include God in two forms. *Enkai* is the creator of the earth. *Enkai-Narok*, the Black God, is found in thunder and rain. He is benevolent and brings love and green pastures. *Enkai-na-Nyokie*, the Red God, is found in lightning and is associated with the dry season. He is vengeful and brings famine. Joseph said the Maasai believe that Enkai sends its believers a guardian spirit to protect them until they die, although they do not believe in an afterlife. And, like many places in Africa and around the world, alongside their traditional beliefs, most Maasai today have also converted to Christianity.

Wealth in this culture is measured by the number of cattle and children they have. The Maasai believe Enkai created cattle especially for his followers, emphasizing the significance of the animals in their lives. All of their food comes from their cattle. They eat the meat, and they drink the milk and the blood, which together are mixed in a gourd called an *ingri*. On my first safari years ago, I brought home a well-used ingri I bought in a village; I was careful to keep the lid on it, as it stunk to high heaven for many, many years. The Maasai's traditional animal protein-based diet keeps them healthy with little evidence of diseases and illness.

The tall and slender Maasai are draped in distinctive, vibrant-red wrap-around cloths. The durable, blanket-like garments protect the herders from harsh weather as they walk distances of up to thirty-five miles in search of green pastures and water sources for their cattle.

In another Maasai village, I visited a school. The area lacks teachers, and because of the nomadic lifestyle, schooling is not the biggest priority, especially for girls. But this is thankfully changing. The Maasai are beginning to see that education is a way to move their culture forward, economically and politically. Joseph explained the Maasai are also learning that education can improve the treatment of women and girls. They are beginning to see how early marriage can stop a girl's schooling in its tracks.

Visiting a classroom

Maasai parents often arrange their daughter's marriage while she's very young, sometimes when she is still an infant. A girl is promised to a man who possesses enough cattle to pay the bride price demanded by her father. Often, she will marry a man much older than herself and will live with the other wives.

Maasai women are known for their beaded jewelry

The women sew elaborate beadwork that is used as everyday jewelry and for special celebrations. Colorful beaded collars, headbands, bracelets, and other pieces represent a person's individual values, such as bravery or fertility, as well as their marital or social status. Heavy earrings embellish their elongated earlobes. I bought a number of bracelets, which I still wear almost every day.

One of the most significant Maasai rituals is circumcision, or *emorata*, which marks a boy's transition to adulthood. Following their circumcision, small groups of Maasai boys will spend four to eight months away from home traveling across their section of land, learning how to become a man and a warrior. They dress in black clothes and paint their faces to keep away the evil spirits. The Maasai are known for their bravery and courage, and as warriors, they will have the responsibility of protecting their homes, villages, and livestock.

Embarking on one of the stages of a rite of passage

And they love to dance.

Celebrations are vital to this culture. Maasai dances are performed for lots of occasions, including to bless the cattle, and for births, weddings, and death. In the Adumu, or "jumping dance," Maasai leap into the air to show their strength and stamina as tribal warriors. Each man will jump as high as he can while the others form a circle around him and sing. They wanted me to join in. I thought they'd be horrified at my jumping ability, but either they were being kind, or I had proven that white girls can indeed jump, even with bad knees.

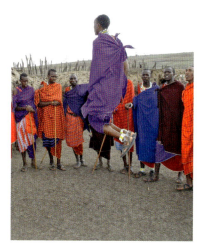

Adumu jumping dance

The Great Rift Valley has some of the most fertile grazing grounds on earth. The Maasai's territory overlaps with the Serengeti plains, which has the highest concentration of predators in Africa as well as the largest herds on the planet.

This greater Serengeti area is renowned for being the path of the Great Migration of two million wildebeest and zebras, one of the world's most amazing wildlife spectacles. Throughout the year, the huge herds move in a clockwise direction around the infinite plains, searching for safe, wet grasslands. There, a whole lot of pregnant wildebeest and zebras will have their babies. The epic journey north covers hundreds of miles. After the rains green up the southern plains, they turn around and come all the way back. Some don't make it, succumbing to fatigue and starvation.

The Great Migration

Watching a migration of this magnitude is mind-blowing! One moment, the massive herds can be grazing and marching together, then, as though something spooked them, they will take off into a roaring stampede. Thousands of animals will rush, sprint, and jump over rivers, all kicking up dust as they flee predators. Sadly, over the years, the plains have become dangerously dry, threatening this incredible migration.

We continued on to the prehistoric Ngorongoro Crater. A volcanic eruption about 2.5 million years ago formed this hundred-square-mile, two-thousand-foot-deep crater. Thirty thousand animals live in it. The day I visited, our biggest sighting was the very rare and endangered black rhino. International groups are working with Tanzania and other African governments to stop wildlife trafficking, but poaching remains a huge threat.

Elephant herds protect their calves.

Despite having lived in Ngorongoro for hundreds of years, today, the Maasai are at risk of being evicted or forced to sell their animals because their livestock interferes with the habitat of the wild animals as well as the development of national parks, which the government relies on for tourism revenue. However, the Maasai are working with the government, conservation groups, and safari businesses to negotiate settlements where everyone can win. The Maasai may not be able to retain land that their ancestors have roamed and farmed for centuries, but they're doing all they can to solve their problems and to cooperate rather than obstruct.

Ngorongoro Crater is the largest caldera in the world.

A solitary man herds his livestock over large areas.

I am so grateful to have circled back to East Africa (where I almost got engaged to James) to spend extended time with the Maasai, a historic tribe of people I first learned about decades earlier. While their unique culture is threatened, the Maasai are resilient. Their ability to persevere under challenging conditions is astonishing, as is their commitment to family and friendship. The fact that they are optimistic about their future is another incredible measure of their character.

In many ways, the Maasai are not much different than other indigenous groups that are clinging to their traditional existence. Global modernization is unavoidable. Absolutely, countries need to provide better access to healthcare and education and bring economic improvement to their people. On the other side, however, are nefarious intentions of those who would line their pockets at the expense of others. We don't have to look far to see unethical—if not illegal—measures, such as farming, mining, forestry, and other commercial development, which claim historic and sacred lands and endanger indigenous cultures.

Tanzania

As President Carter said, "We must adjust to changing times and still hold on to unchanging principles."

As I travel, I am continually awed by those doing all they can to keep their cultures alive: not only indigenous groups, but people everywhere who look to their elders and ancestors for wisdom and guidance, who turn to their religion and spirituality for courage and hope, and who work alongside local leaders to find common ground and solve problems.

If we are facing the right direction, a Buddhist proverb says, *all we have to do is keep on walking.*

Never underestimate the human spirit.

Peace

CLOSE

If I Could Visit My Younger Self

Growing up, I wasn't sure where I fit in or whether I'd fit in at all. But if I could tell my younger self anything, if I could visit my younger self now, I'd have a whole lot to share.

First of all, younger self, you're not the only one with questions, fears, and trepidations about the future. You're not alone. As a new graduate, you naturally will be asked by everyone, what's next, what are you going to do (like, with your life)? These questions are not realistic, and they're not even fair. How can any young person who doesn't yet have much life experience be expected to make big decisions that may affect the rest of their life? So, don't worry about it. Goals are good, and many of your friends may know where they want to go to college and what they want to do next. Good for them. But not everybody knows that, not yet.

Tons of your friends will decide to get married and have kids. Not that there's anything wrong with that, but you don't have to do what

Opening My Cultural Lens

others do. (Dad always said that. He was wise, and he was right.) Take your time because you'll find that being single offers a bounty of opportunities in just about every aspect of life, including work, community, relationships, and travel.

You're going to meet a lot of talented, career-driven people, many of whom will become very successful. But here's something to chew on: just because you're good at something or because a job pays well, it may not be satisfying, it may not make you happy. As you grow and spread your wings, you will discover new interests and involvements and form new relationships, all of which will help you find your place. You will learn how important it is to enjoy what you do because that will become your measure of success.

One of the greatest aspects of good health is humor. So, laugh a lot. And always be kind. (Mom will always be remembered for the kindness she showed throughout her life—what a legacy.) Remember some of the other things your parents taught you. Be accountable. If you say you're going to do something, do it. Show respect to others by being on time and returning messages promptly. That will serve you well. Oh—and wear sensible shoes.

Spend time with those you respect and regard, and with those who bring joy and positive energy. It's contagious. Broaden your circle of friends to include those who are interesting, those you admire. Take some risks. Sure, you'll get some bad breaks and make some stupid mistakes, but you'll also get lucky. Take the luck. And if something really matters to you, if you really want to do something, do it as early as you can because life sometimes gets in the way. The five worst words are: I wish I would have.

Finally, embrace your curiosity. It's one of our greatest human qualities. Stretch outside your comfort zone (it won't hurt). Seek out new people whose backgrounds, religions, and traditions are different from yours. Along the way, you also may begin to find your spiritual path, one that provides ethical principles and moral guidance. And always be grateful for family and friends who encourage you, and for strangers who inspire you. Let them know it.

You're going to meet so many intriguing people and do more incredible things than ever appeared in your dreams. Each new discovery will challenge your assumptions and will help to dismantle your biases. These experiences will help you—and others—to understand that people are more alike than different.

Opening your aperture to a diverse world will profoundly influence who you want to be and who you will become. It also will increase your confidence and self-worth. You will fit in.

Enjoy the ride. It'll be a blast. You will be flabbergasted at where it will take you. And who knows, maybe you'll even jump out of an airplane someday.

Happy trails!

A leap of faith at 14,000 feet

Acknowledgments

For years and years, my friends would ask me, "when are you going to do something with all your photos, and when in the world are you going to write a darn coffee table book?" I honestly had little bandwidth to take on such a project. Still, I loved returning from my trips and putting together scripted slide presentations about my adventures that I'd share with hundreds of friends, colleagues, and strangers. These annual trips and subsequent slide shows were the highlights of my year. I loved sharing my experiences about captivating and unique places that opened others' eyes to the world. So, I continued to travel to places where I could witness those kinds of cultures—mostly remote, some isolated, and many at risk from modernization and development.

And then came Covid-19.

We will forever tell stories about how the pandemic affected us—our families and jobs, our friends and social lives. But had it

Opening My Cultural Lens

not been for the lockdown, I never would have carved out the time to write a book. It was now or never. But while planning a coffee table book, I soon realized I instead needed to write a full-blown account of many of my trips, not just a photo book. Luckily, I still had all my scripts from decades of slideshows and presentations. My notes were not lost. And so, I began to write a *book*—a personal story about how my global cultural adventures completely and irreversibly influenced my life.

The project—which is actually an extension of my cultural education work—allowed me to record my experiences on paper, primarily for myself, my family, and a lot of friends who have followed my journeys for decades. It also gave me the opportunity to answer a lot of questions I'm asked all the time: what got you interested in cultural travel? Who plans your trips? What's your favorite place? Were you ever afraid? What have you learned? And most meaningfully, how has it changed you?

I could not have accomplished this project if it weren't for many of you. Your sincere interest and insistence made me believe this all was possible. You've followed my escapades, looked at my photos, and watched my videos. To all of you who came to my slide shows, presentations, speeches, art fairs, and gallery exhibits, thank you. And to those who now pay closer attention to current events, geography, history, social justice, and human rights—thank you for listening, watching, and sharing. There are too many of you to name, and if I tried, I would be devastated to learn I had omitted someone. You know who you are. I can never repay you all for your love, friendship, and support.

I'm also indebted to my many clients, who never blinked an eye when I told them where I was off to next and how long I'd be gone. Without your unwavering support, my trips would not have been possible.

For dozens of years, Preferred Adventures coordinated my trips and connected me with world-class resources. Most importantly, they helped assign my guides—cultural experts who are all regarded in their respective circles and neighborhoods. These guides knew local families, community leaders, shamans, imams, village chiefs, medicine men, and a few good headhunters. My guides introduced me to worlds beyond my dreams. They also steered me away from danger. Without hesitation, I literally trusted them with my life, including the wild bush pilots that plunged us into carved out runways in the middle of nowhere. My guides were my lifeline. We also shared stories about our backgrounds, families, traditions, and religions. And we laughed!

My profound appreciation goes to my Cultural Jambalaya family and to those who guided me in 2005, at the very beginning, to help form the nonprofit: Rayla, Pat, Colleen, Christine, James, Kevin, and Jen; and to my amazing current board, and many other dedicated former board members and advisors, as well as countless volunteers, sponsors, partners, and donors of our work. Again, there are too many to thank. You have helped us blossom from providing free educational content for teachers in Minnesota, to reaching millions of students in classrooms around the country and the world. I am forever grateful.

After a few months of writing, I met with Terri Foley, a friend who has experience in editing and publishing, and who provided early guidance that helped shape the book. But had it not been for Beth Hawkins, the book never would've gotten off the ground. She edited each chapter to help get the manuscript ready to present to a publisher. I cannot adequately express my gratitude.

And, thanks to my publisher, Beaver's Pond Press, particularly Laurie Buss Herrmann, managing editor; Kerry Stapley, content editor; and Dan Pitts, designer. Having never done anything like this before, you made it so easy. You expertly guided me through an otherwise daunting process, all the while polishing the stories, layout, and design. I could not have done this without you.

I save this part for last because it's the most important. Nothing can happen without family. I am enormously grateful for the love and support of my brother's crazy clan, and for my wonderful cousins. But I so wish my parents were around today to see how my career, nonprofit, and frankly, my life, have evolved. I also wish they could have read this book. I think they would have enjoyed learning about my experiences. I think they'd be happy, and perhaps, a bit relieved to see how that young Milwaukee girl turned out.

My immediate family is small—just my brother, Bill, and sister, Jean. We are extremely close. Bill lives in Milwaukee, and I miss him more than one can imagine. We are cut from the same cloth, and even though I can't see him often enough, he is in my thoughts, heart—and jokes—all the time.

Yet I am so fortunate and blessed to have Jean in my life every single day. For decades, she has encouraged me and has been a partner and champion in my endeavors. Having her support has helped me realize my goals, ambitions, and indeed—my dreams, which ultimately have transformed my passion into purpose.

I love you all to the moon, which, by the way, is where I want to go next!

All dressed up and ready to go

Discussion Questions

1. Gail repeatedly makes the point that we're more alike than different. Do you agree with her? Why or why not?

2. Gail makes the distinction that she is a cultural traveler, *not* a tourist. What do you think the difference is? What are some ways that we can cultivate our own cultural-traveler mindset when we visit new people and places, at home or abroad?

3. Gail's journeys brought her face-to-face with hundreds of people whose backgrounds, languages, traditions, and religions were vastly different from her own. Have Gail's experiences inspired you to think differently about other peoples' lives and cultures?

4. Which countries or cultures surprised you the most? Did you think these places would be better or worse than Gail's experiences of them? What led to your previous beliefs, and what was it about Gail's experiences that caused those beliefs to change?

Opening My Cultural Lens

5. If you could bring one aspect of another culture into your own life, what would it be?

6. Gail feels she can better understand a place by learning about its history. What do you think our ongoing relationship with human history should be? How impactful should we let our history be on our modern lives?

7. In the chapter on Namibia, an elder said, "Our life is good. We have no fighting, no crime, no hunger, and no hatred. We are satisfied. Do you live as well in your land?" What do you think of his assessment, and how do you think the quality of our modernized lives compares to his own? What has been gained and what has been lost through modernization? Have our advancements made us happier?

8. Nearly all of Gail's guides were men. How do you think Gail's travels—her experiences and impressions—might have differed if women had been guiding these trips instead?

9. Gail devoted decades of her life to exploring remote and distant cultures. Do you think she found what she was looking for?